Woman's Day
Snack Cookbook

Woman's Day Snack Cookbook

by Lyn Stallworth

 A Media Projects Incorporated Book

COLLIER BOOKS
A Division of Macmillan Publishing Co., Inc.
New York

COLLIER MACMILLAN PUBLISHERS
London

Macmillan Publishing Co., Inc.
866 Third Avenue, New York, N.Y. 10022
Collier Macmillan Canada, Ltd.

Library of Congress Cataloging in
Publication Data
Stallworth, Lyn.
    Woman's day snack cookbook.
    Includes index.
    1. Snack foods.
    I. Woman's day. II. Title.
TX740.S73   641.5'3   80-10105
ISBN 0-02-613550-7
ISBN 0-02-009820-0-pbk

First Collier Books Edition 1980

Woman's Day Snack Cookbook is also
published in
a hardcover edition by Macmillan
Publishing Co., Inc.

Created by Media Projects Incorporated.

Photography by Sally Andersen-Bruce.

Printed in the United States of America

Contents

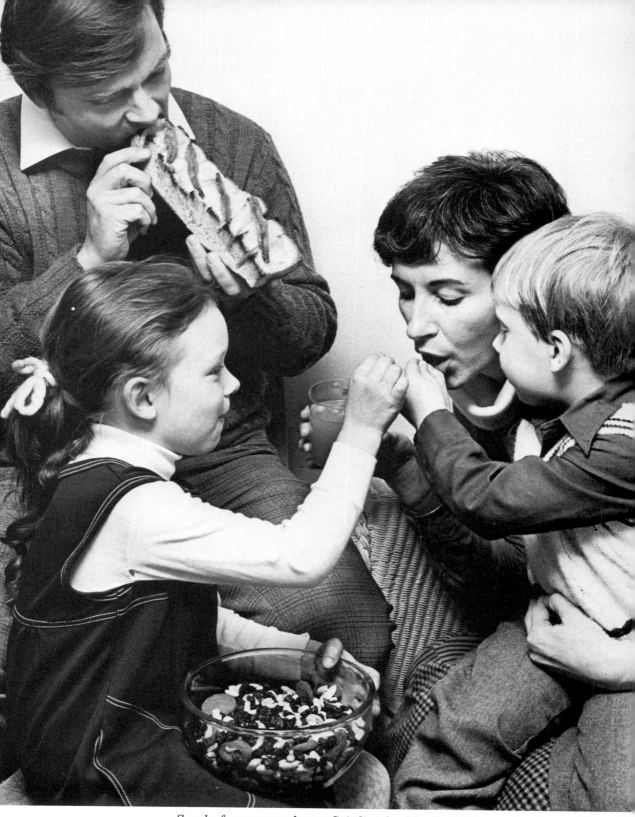

Snacks for everyone: hearty Spiedini, healthy Trail Mix, cooling Orange Blush.

Introduction

"Time for a little something." That's Winnie the Pooh speaking, and every snacker struck by a sudden craving knows exactly what he means. In Pooh's case the "little something" is always a pot of honey, but then he is a bear of little brain. Humans in search of a treat come up with many more interesting snacks, from nut-and-raisin "gorp" to a chunk of Spiedini dripping with cheese and fragrant with anchovies. Because a snack to the yogurt gulper on the run is so different from the teen-ager's snack—which might look suspiciously like a whole meal—it is hard to define what a snack is in general terms. What is there in common between a chocolate sundae, a Soy Chicken Wing, and granola?

Time, for one thing. When the snacking urge strikes, it demands prompt satisfaction. Maybe—just maybe—you can wait a half hour. More likely, the limit is 10 minutes. Almost all the recipes here (the exceptions are snacks to make ahead of urge and keep on hand) can be made in from 1 to 30 minutes, whether they are as light as a Stuffed Egg or as hearty as pasta with Seven-Minute Tomato Sauce. Speed of preparation, however, doesn't come close to defining a snack. There's a quirkiness of taste, a yen for the warmth of spiced melted cheese, for the comfort of chocolate, the bite of hot peppers, the indulgence of butter and garlic and juicy meat. And the crunch of nuts, the crisp greens, the creamy dips, chewy candy, a cooling drink. And more—jam oozing from a golden crepe, Tiny Toast Cups heaped with pink Potted Shrimp, bubbling mellow Welsh Rarebit over a juicy grilled tomato, nibbles of Pork Cubes, a handful of popcorn, a single tiny meatball balanced on a toothpick. There are snacks for you!

You needn't wait for mealtime—half the pleasure of a snack is that it is food to be sipped, munched, crunched, at just the right time—which is anytime you feel like it.

Of course, the essence of a snack is that it is an indulgence; and for that reason many feel that snacking is neither in the moral nor the nutritional realm of three square meals a day. Morally, be assured that if you feel snacking is a sin, all the world is in it together. While you sneak a snack of tuna salad, the Turks sip Ayran, the Chinese whip up an Egg Fu Yung, the Greeks pop Keftedakia into their mouths, the Caribbean islanders munch Plantain Chips, and the English celebrate tea with scones.

Nutritionally, you have nothing at all to worry about. What could be more nutritious than the basic foods: cheese and eggs, yogurt, fresh fruits, fresh vegetables, wholesome grains, beans, and meats? That the basics are shaped prettily, seasoned imaginatively, and served in snack-sized portions injures none of the vitamins, minerals, and proteins nature has endowed them with. For the dieter, of course, quantity and calories do make a difference. In every chapter—even Sweets—dieters will find tasty recipes to suit their needs and cravings.

So will everyone else. This book is organized to help each person find the right dish for just that moment, just that craving. A really "little something" will be found in Tidbits and Dips; more substantial foods in Solid Satisfactions. If you know for sure your mood calls for a warming soup, or your refrigerator has nothing to offer but an egg, there are chapters on both. If the only image you can summon to mind is a vague idea like "crisp," or "highly seasoned," or "sweet," look in the special index that categorizes recipes by craving. Certain people have very specific snacking needs: the hiker for snacks that keep well, travel light, and pack a nutritional wallop; the parent for snacks children can prepare after school; the host or hostess for sophisticated international snacks that make a memorable cocktail party; and all of us for snack menus that, after a long day, can substitute for supper. Features that offer suggestions for these and many other special snacking needs are scattered throughout the book, wherever they might be most helpful.

Many recipes in this book suggest substitutions and variations. Use them when you haven't just the right ingredients, or use them because you crave a novel flavor or an unusual texture. Or ignore our suggestions, and experiment on your own. There is no snacking elite that can claim peanut butter on a banana slice is an outrage or a vulgarity. There is no authority on the uses of catsup or the insides of pita pockets. The indulgence of snacking is that it has no rules: no standard cuisine; no set places, times, or courses; no limits.

The Snacker's Pantry

The snacking urge has no respect for business hours. It can strike long after the stores have closed, and you are missing the one ingredient you crave. You can't of course keep a supermarket-sized inventory on limited shelf space, but the modest Snacker's Pantry below should get you through many an off-hour urge. The list of canned, dried, and bottled ingredients are those most often needed for the recipes in this book. You will also find, in the introduction to each section, other suggestions for ready-to-eat snacks you may want to keep on hand. And the usual staples—dairy products, dry ingredients, fresh lemons and garlic, a useful cheese such as cheddar—should be kept in stock, too.

Crackers, any favorite variety
Nuts, salted, dry-roasted, or raw
Dried fruits, such as raisins, apricots, apples
Small cans of fruit, any favorite variety
Small cans of vegetables, especially those useful in salads such as kidney beans, chick-peas, bean sprouts, artichoke hearts, beets
Fish, such as tuna, sardines, anchovies
Pasta, any favorite variety
Canned whole tomatoes
Broth, beef or chicken, canned or soup cubes
Dried herbs, particularly thyme, oregano, basil, mustard, and dill
Chili powder
Curry powder
Grated Parmesan cheese
Catsup or chili sauce
Worcestershire sauce
Soy sauce, preferably imported
Hot-pepper sauce
Prepared horseradish
Mustard, spicy brown or Dijon
Olives, green and ripe
Pickles and relishes, any favorite varieties
Capers
Pimientos

Popping corn for Parmesan Popcorn.

CHAPTER ONE
Tidbits & Dips

These are bite-size snacks, to pop into the mouth by the bit or by the bunch. Knives, forks, and spoons are definitely out; hands are in. On the whole, tidbits and dips satisfy a craving for something crunchy, often with the added tang of salt and the delight of unusual flavors.

Tidbit and dip snackers will want to keep commercial products on hand. It's not easy to keep pretzels, potato chips, crackers, and nuts in optimum condition. Time and humidity are the enemies. Oils break down and become rancid (this is especially true of shelled nuts) and unless you live in the desert, dampness is always a problem. There are, however, some measures you can take to prolong crispness and flavor. Transfer opened crackers, chips, and pretzels to airtight tins or jars. When they are empty, wash and dry them well before refilling. Store nuts in the freezer, packed in tightly capped jars. Limp, but not yet stale, crackers, chips, and so on can be recrisped by 20 minutes or so in a 200-degree oven. Spread them on a baking sheet; watch carefully for signs of scorching.

Another idea for nut and cracker lovers is to make small amounts of nut butters. Peanuts are an old favorite, but cashews and almonds make more delicate butters. A blender is all that's needed. Use roasted, salted nuts, a handful at a time, and blend to the consistency you prefer.

All the world seems to have a taste for crunchiness. Two imported snacks to try are Chinese shrimp chips and the Indian wafers called popadums. Both keep well in the refrigerator or in the pantry; you fry them as you want them in oil. They are fun to prepare, too; deep-fried shrimp chips swell enormously in a second. Popadums, slid into a small amount of hot oil in a heavy skillet, sizzle and grow in the twinkling of an eye. Flip them with tongs to the other side to brown for a moment, drain on paper, and you have a marvelous warm, crunchy tidbit.

Trail Mix

Variations on this theme are known in some areas as "gorp"—good old raisins and peanuts. No matter what its name, this snack is excellent and nutritious. Nor is it just for hikers; children also like to make it, and, I might add, eat it. Use the type of nuts—dry roasted, unsalted, or roasted and salted—you prefer. They all blend well in this mix.

Unsalted pumpkin seeds
Unsalted sunflower seeds
Walnut halves
Pecans
Cashews
Peanuts
Packaged sweetened shredded coconut
Raisins or currants
Dried fruit, such as apples, apricots, or peaches, cut into ½-inch bits
Semisweet chocolate bits (optional)

Mix together equal amounts—about ⅓ cup—of all or most of the ingredients. Trail Mix keeps, tightly covered in jars, for up to a week, or if refrigerated, 2–3 weeks.

Almond Granola

3 cups uncooked old-fashioned rolled oats
1½ cups packaged shredded coconut, preferably unsweetened
½ cup wheat germ
1 cup sunflower seeds
¼ cup sesame seeds
¼ cup vegetable oil
½ cup honey
½ cup cold water

1 cup slivered blanched almonds
½ cup raisins or chopped dried fruit

Preheat the oven to 225 degrees. In a large bowl mix together the first 5 ingredients. Add the oil, honey, and water, and mix thoroughly. Spread the mixture out in a large oiled jelly-roll pan and bake in the oven, stirring frequently, for 1½ hours. Add the almonds and continue baking, stirring frequently, for 1 hour more, or until the granola is dry, lightly browned, and crisp. Mix in the raisins or fruit bits. Store in airtight containers. Makes about 5 cups.

Chili Nut Crunch

Chili Nut Crunch keeps stored for a week. However, that's seldom a problem: it's usually all gobbled up in a day or two.

3 cups bite-size shredded-wheat cereal
3 cups bite-size shredded-corn cereal
1 cup mixed roasted, salted nuts
2 cups pretzel sticks
½ cup butter or margarine
3 tablespoons Worcestershire sauce
1 teaspoon chili powder
1 teaspoon ground cumin
½ teaspoon salt or seasoned salt

Preheat the oven to 250 degrees. In a large shallow baking pan, spread the wheat and corn cereal, nuts, and pretzel sticks and heat them on the middle rack of the oven for 5 minutes. Melt the butter or margarine, add the Worcestershire sauce, chili powder, cumin, and salt and pour the mixture over the cereal mixture, turning it with a spoon to coat it evenly. Bake the mix for 45 minutes, stirring every 15 minutes. Spread the crunch on paper towels to drain and cool. Serve in a bowl or store in airtight containers. Makes 9 cups.

Roast Pumpkin Seeds

Once a year—and only once—a family with children finds itself with the makings for an old-fashioned snack of roast pumpkin seeds. The trick is to get a large pumpkin, the skin of which is quite hard to dent with a fingernail. The treat is that the seeds in a ripe pumpkin are numerous, large, and plump.

After the pumpkin has been opened and the pulp removed, separate the seeds from the pulp as best you can. Shreds of pumpkin will still cling to many of them. Empty the seeds into a colander, and put the colander partly under running water in the sink. With your fingers, remove pumpkin shreds from the seeds, then scoop them from the colander and lay them on paper towels to drain.

When the seeds are dry, spread them in a baking pan, add a tablespoon or two of butter or margarine, and sprinkle them with salt. Roast the seeds in the oven at 300 degrees for about an hour, stirring frequently. The seeds are done when they are golden brown. They can be eaten warm, but make a crunchy, toasty snack at room temperature, too.

Pumpkin cleaning is a messy job. Indoors, spread today's newspaper under and around the pumpkin to protect surroundings, keep seeds from getting dirty, and make clean-up easier.

Wheat-Walnut Savory

½ cup butter or margarine
1 tablespoon Worcestershire sauce, or to taste
4 cups bite-size shredded-wheat cereal
2 cups coarsely chopped walnuts
1 teaspoon salt, or to taste

Preheat the oven to 350 degrees. In a large roasting pan melt the butter or margarine in the oven, remove the pan, and blend in the Worcestershire sauce. Add the wheat cereal and walnuts, turning them to coat them evenly, and sprinkle the mixture with salt. Bake the savory for 20 minutes, stirring it thoroughly 2 or 3 times and adding more salt, if desired. Serve the savory immediately or store it for a few days in airtight containers. Makes 6 cups.

Parmesan Popcorn

Pop popcorn according to the directions on the package and pour enough melted butter or margarine over it to coat each kernel. Tip the popcorn into a paper bag and add enough grated Parmesan or Romano cheese to coat it. Shake the bag vigorously; pour the popcorn into a bowl, and serve.

Cinnamon Popcorn

Prepare popcorn as above, but add to the bag brown sugar mixed with a liberal sprinkling of cinnamon instead of cheese. Shake vigorously and serve.

Plantain Chips

Plantains are found in Latin and Caribbean markets. They resemble large bananas, but must be cooked to be edible.

1 ripe, but not completely blackened plantain,
peeled and cut into ¼-inch diagonal slices
Vegetable oil

In a skillet gently fry the plantain slices in ¼-inch hot vegetable oil for about 2 minutes on each side. With a slotted spoon remove the chips and place them between 2 sheets of waxed paper. Reserve the oil. With a rolling pin, flatten the chips. (You may prepare plantain chips several hours in advance to this point. If doing so, store them between the sheets of waxed paper in the refrigerator. The second frying will, of course, take slightly longer.) Reheat the oil and return the chips to the skillet. Refry them for about 30 seconds on each side or until they are golden brown. Drain the chips on paper towels and serve immediately. Makes about 1 dozen.

Chewy Pork Cubes

Some of the best food is simplicity itself, and pork cubes are an example of this. They are equally good warm or cold.

> ½ pound lean pork shoulder or tenderloin,
>   trimmed and cut into ¼-inch cubes
> 1 teaspoon salt
> Pepper

Preheat the oven to 200 degrees. Season the pork cubes with salt and pepper on all sides and spread them out on a baking sheet. Roast the cubes on the middle rack of the oven for 1½ hours, or until they are crisp. Makes about 3 dozen.

Beef Jerky

> Round steak trimmed of all fat and gristle, cut
>   along the grain into ⅛-inch slices
> Salt

In a bowl sprinkle the beef liberally with salt and let it stand, stirring 2 or 3 times, for 1 hour. Preheat the oven to 250 degrees. Hang the slices, 1 inch apart, on long barbecue skewers. Hang the skewers with S-hooks (available at hardware stores) from the top rack of the oven. Or, starting with a cold oven, lay the skewers on the top rack and let the strips of beef hang down between the rack wires. Put a pan in the bottom of the oven to catch the drippings. Bake the beef for 3 to

4 hours, or until it is dark and dry. Store the jerky in jars in the refrigerator or freeze it in plastic bags.

Anchovy Toast

This puree may be chilled, covered, and used on crackers, preferably low in salt, as well as on toast.

> 1 2-ounce tin flat anchovies, drained
> 2 tablespoons butter or margarine, softened
> Cayenne or hot-pepper sauce to taste
> Lemon juice to taste
> Lightly toasted bread, crusts removed

In a food processor fitted with the metal blade, or by hand, puree the anchovies with the butter or margarine and add cayenne or hot-pepper sauce and lemon juice to taste. Spread the puree on toast and broil the toast until the butter sizzles. Makes ¼ cup puree.

Pie Crust Cheese Straws

> ½ package (5 ounces) pie crust mix
> ¼ cup shredded cheddar or Swiss cheese, or crumbled blue cheese

Preheat the oven to 425 degrees. Prepare the dough according to the directions on the package and roll it out on a floured board into a rectangle. Sprinkle the top half of the rectangle with cheese. Fold the bottom half over the top half and roll the dough out again into a rectangle about ¼-inch thick. Cut the dough into strips, 3 inches long and ½-inch wide, and place them on a lightly buttered baking sheet. Bake the straws on the middle rack of the oven for 10 to 12 minutes. Straws keep for several days in a tightly covered container. Makes about 2 dozen.

Curry Straws

Prepare a rectangle of dough, as in the recipe above, but sprinkle half of it with 1 teaspoon curry powder. Roll the dough out again, cut it, and bake and store the straws as in the master recipe.

Sesame Straws

Roll out a large rectangle of dough and sprinkle it with 2 tablespoons sesame seeds. Lightly press the seeds into the dough. Do not roll out the dough again, but cut it into strips and proceed with the master recipe.

Wheaten Cheese Crackers

2 cups minus 2 tablespoons flour
¼ teaspoon baking soda
½ teaspoon salt
½ cup yellow cornmeal, preferably stone-ground
¼ cup wheat germ
½ cup butter or margarine
1 cup shredded sharp cheddar cheese
½ cup milk
1 tablespoon white vinegar

Preheat the oven to 375 degrees. In a large bowl combine the flour, baking soda, salt, cornmeal, and wheat germ and cut in the butter or margarine until the mixture resembles coarse meal. Stir in the cheese. Combine the milk and vinegar and add the mixture to the dry ingredients. Mix lightly until the liquids are just absorbed. On a lightly floured board knead the dough for 2 minutes, or until it holds together, and roll it out ⅛-inch thick. Cut the dough into 2¼-by-1¼-inch rectangles and prick them with a fork. Sprinkle the rectangles with additional wheat germ if desired and put them on lightly greased baking sheets. Bake the crackers for 12 to 15 minutes and cool them on racks. Makes about 6 dozen.

Backpack Snacks

Backpack snacks are lightweight, high-energy foods especially good for the hiker, the biker, the cross-country skier, the bird watcher. People on strenuous outings can't be encumbered with bulky hampers or lots of Thermos bottles, so these snacks should also be designed to be eaten with a minimum of utensils or mess. Trail Mix is an excellent backpack snack. Its dried fruits contain sugars that can be digested within minutes to give the quick energy strenuous activity requires. The nuts are high in protein.

Other lightweight, space-saving, non-messy, and highly nutritious foods include dried meats, such as Pork Cubes and Beef Jerky. Except for its weight, fresh fruit is a fine active snack as well. Choose non-squishy fruit like apples or oranges, and plan to eat it at your first stop.

You may want to supplement the snacks you make with a few store-bought items. Supermarkets sell dried sausages, concentrated breakfast squares, and health food bars. Sporting goods stores often have a line of dehydrated foods. They are expensive, but for long excursions the convenience and minimal weight justify the price. It's a good idea to carry a few packets of saturated towels to wipe your hands before and after eating.

To keep at the peak of your form as you exercise, how you eat is as important as what you eat. Keep amounts small—a full stomach may be no problem on an ordinary picnic where you can sleep off a complete meal under a tree before driving home, but that bloated feeling is no fun on a bike tour. Eat those small amounts frequently, to keep your body supplied with food. Snacks like dried fruit—prunes, pears, apricots, and apples—or a handful of Trail Mix, can be kept in your pocket so that you can munch as you walk, ride, or ski.

When packing snacks, bear in mind the "jiggle" factor. Food carried in a backpack or bike bag shakes loose. Wrap food in a plastic bag, tie it, then place that bag inside another one and tie it.

If you know you'll run across a water supply and the means to heat it, pack bouillon cubes, instant coffee and sugar in packets, and tea bags. Pack a pair of foam cups, one wedged inside the other for strength. In hot weather take packets of iced tea and lemonade mix. If no water will be available, do as cross-country skiers do—sling a leather bag filled with water, wine, or fruit juice over your shoulder.

Stuffed Snack Loaf

Here's a solution to canapés for a crowd. The taste is smooth yet zingy, and thin slices of the loaf have a professional catered look. A processor makes the job easy, but if you don't have one, crumble the bread with your fingers, puree the vegetables in a blender, and cream together, at room temperature, the remaining ingredients. Proportions are given for a very large loaf of bread. If you reduce the recipe, keep in mind that you need twice as much cream cheese as liverwurst.

> 1 large loaf crusty French or Italian bread,
>   about 18 inches long
> ¼ cup chopped parsley
> ¼ cup chopped radishes
> ¼ cup chopped onion
> ½ pound liverwurst
> 2 8-ounce packages cream cheese
> 3 tablespoons beer or cream
> ½ teaspoon Worcestershire sauce
> 1 tablespoon dry mustard

Preheat the oven to 350 degrees. Cut the ends off the loaf and cut the loaf into thirds. Scoop out as much of the inside of the bread as you can and crumble it in a food processor fitted with the metal blade. On a baking sheet, toast the crumbs on the middle rack of the oven for 15 minutes, or until dry and lightly browned, and let them cool. In the processor puree each vegetable separately and transfer it to a large mixing bowl. Without cleaning out the processor, add the liverwurst, cream cheese, beer or cream, Worcestershire sauce, and mustard and blend the mixture to a smooth paste. Transfer the paste to the vegetables, add the crumbs, and fold them together. Set the hollowed-out bread sections on end and stuff them with the mixture. Wrap each section in plastic wrap or foil and chill them at least 6 hours. Better still, half-freeze them; this takes only about an hour and allows you to cut the thinnest possible slices.

Crudités (Raw Vegetables)

Keep an assortment of washed and prepared raw vegetables—carrot, celery, zucchini, or cucumber sticks; radishes;

Jerusalem artichokes; cauliflower or broccoli flowerets; cherry tomatoes—in the crisper of the refrigerator. With a sour cream dip, they make fine snacks.

½ cup sour cream
1 tablespoon prepared horseradish
½ teaspoon seasoned salt
2 cups assorted raw vegetables, cut into bite-size
  pieces

In a bowl, mix all ingredients except the vegetables well and chill them, covered. Serve as a dip with the cut-up vegetables. Makes ½ cup.

Cheese-Olive Spread

This spread is also a winner as a filler for celery stalks or endive leaves.

1 3-ounce package cream cheese, softened
¼ cup crumbled blue cheese
¾ cup coarsely chopped pitted black olives
2 tablespoons mayonnaise
¼ cup minced celery

In a bowl cream the cream cheese together with the blue cheese and mix in the remaining ingredients. Makes 1½ cups.

Cheese-Pineapple Spread

1 8-ounce package cream cheese, softened
1 teaspoon ground ginger
3 ounces blue cheese, crumbled
⅓ cup crushed pineapple, drained
⅓ cup chopped pecans
Chopped parsley

Cream the cream cheese together with the ginger until the cheese is fluffy. Blend in the blue cheese and stir in the pineapple and pecans. Serve the spread sprinkled with chopped parsley. Makes 2 cups.

The TV Crowd

In these liberated times few women—or men, for that matter—are willing to confine themselves to the kitchen preparing trays of tidbits for a gang glued to the tube in the living room. It's everyone's right to be there watching the Big Game or the election returns, and that includes the folks who provide the video-side box seats.

But as every host and hostess who invite the TV crowd in know, all that on-screen action builds up a powerful case of the munchies in the viewers. For reasons unknown to medical science the watchers get hungrier than the performers. The nib-

blers turn into gobblers, the gobblers outdo themselves, and several nut dishes are emptied before the first commercial. To keep everyone happy, a lot of food should be provided, but none of it should be the sort that takes anyone away from the action for long. Salty snacks belong at a television party; they're the perfect accompaniment to beer or soft drinks. Dips, particularly the more savory ones such as Beer Cheese or Liptauer Cheese Pot, are satisfying midnight fillers. And if that is not enough, prepare ahead of time the really substantial Canapé Loaf.

Tzatziki
(Greek Yogurt and Cucumber Dip)

2 cups plain yogurt
1 large cucumber, peeled, seeded, and grated
1 to 3 cloves garlic, finely chopped, or ⅓ cup
    chopped green onions, including some of the
    green tops
2 tablespoons chopped parsley
Salt
Pepper to taste

Drain the yogurt in a fine sieve set over a bowl. If the yogurt is very thin, line the sieve with a double layer of rinsed cheesecloth. Depending on how stiff (dense) you want the yogurt, let it drain for 30 minutes to overnight in the refrigerator. If it becomes too stiff, beat some of the drained liquid back in.

In a bowl toss the cucumber with salt and let it stand to exude water for 30 minutes or overnight in the refrigerator. Squeeze out the cucumber and add it to the yogurt with the garlic or green onions, the pepper, and most of the parsley. Add salt and pepper to taste and sprinkle the dip with the remaining parsley. Serve at once, or cover with plastic wrap and refrigerate for up to 24 hours. Let the Tzatziki return to room temperature before serving. Makes about 3 cups.

Liptauer Cheese Pot

Here's one of those recipes that tastes so very much better than it reads.

8 ounces cottage cheese
½ cup butter or margarine, softened
1 tablespoon paprika, preferably sweet imported
    Hungarian
Pepper to taste
¼ teaspoon salt, or to taste
2 teaspoons caraway seeds
1 teaspoon dry mustard
1 tablespoon finely chopped or grated onion
½ cup sour cream

Rub the cottage cheese through a sieve into a bowl or blend it with an electric mixer until it is smooth. In a bowl cream the butter or margarine and beat in the cottage cheese, paprika, pepper, salt, caraway seeds, mustard, onion, and sour cream. Beat the mixture until it forms a smooth paste. Serve Liptauer cheese on crackers or toast. It keeps up to a week in jars in the refrigerator and improves in flavor as it ages. Makes about 2 cups.

Beer Cheese

½ teaspoon finely chopped garlic
1 tablespoon Worcestershire sauce
½ teaspoon hot-pepper sauce
1 teaspoon dry mustard
½ teaspoon salt, or to taste
1 cup beer
4 cups (about 1 pound) shredded sharp cheddar cheese

In a large bowl mash the garlic to a paste with the back of a spoon, beat in the Worcestershire sauce, hot-pepper sauce, mustard, and salt. Pour the beer in slowly, blending the ingredients, and beat in the cheese, 1 cupful at a time. Continue to beat the mixture until it is smooth. Beer cheese can also be made in a food processor. With the metal blade blend the garlic, Worcestershire sauce, hot pepper sauce, mustard, and salt and add the cheese, 1 cupful at a time. Store beer cheese, covered, in a jar and chill it for 12 to 24 hours to blend the flavors. Makes 2 cups.

Hummus Bi Tahini
(Chick-pea and Sesame Paste Puree)

A food processor or blender makes this classic Middle Eastern spread a snap, without all the mashing, pounding, and pulverizing of the classic method. The sesame paste, called tahini, is sold in Middle Eastern markets, many supermarkets, and health food stores. Hummus also makes an interesting sauce on hamburgers or lamb patties.

1 10½-ounce can chick-peas (ceci or garbanzos),
  drained in a sieve and rinsed under cold run-
  ning water
2 medium cloves garlic, coarsely chopped
½ cup tahini
1 teaspoon salt
¼ cup water
1 tablespoon lemon juice, or to taste
Paprika

In a food processor fitted with the metal blade or in a blender, puree all the ingredients except paprika, scraping down the sides of the container with a rubber spatula. Add more water if necessary; hummus should be thin enough to spread easily. Serve hummus, dusted with paprika, in a shallow bowl. To eat, scoop it up with bits of toasted pita bread. Hummus keeps for several days, covered with plastic wrap, in the refrigerator. Makes 1½ cups.

Guacamole
(Mexican Avocado Dip)

Here is a winter version of guacamole. In summer, when fine ripe tomatoes are available, gently fold in half a large one, peeled, seeded, and coarsely chopped.

1 large ripe avocado
1 tablespoon lemon juice, or to taste
2 tablespoons finely chopped or grated onion
½ teaspoon salt
½ teaspoon ground cumin
½ canned jalapeño pepper, seeded and finely
  chopped, or a few drops hot-pepper sauce

Halve, peel, and pit the avocado and in a bowl combine the pulp with lemon juice to keep the pulp from darkening. Add the remaining ingredients and mash them well. Add more salt if necessary. Serve guacamole immediately with crackers or taco chips. Makes about 1 cup.

Ham and Egg Butter

1 cup cooked ham
3 hard-cooked egg yolks
½ cup butter or margarine softened
1 teaspoon paprika

In a food processor fitted with the metal blade or in a blender, grind the ham and add the remaining ingredients, blending them well. (If making by hand, grind the ham in a meat grinder, sieve the yolks into a bowl, and add the butter or margarine, paprika, and ham, beating.) Serve the butter on crackers or Melba toast, or stuff it into hard-cooked egg halves, p. 53, or Tiny Toast Cups, p. 16. Makes 1¼ cups.

Tiny Toast Cups

Make these little shells when you have the time, and freeze them.

12 very thin slices white bread
3 tablespoons butter or margarine, melted

Preheat the oven to 375 degrees. With a rolling pin flatten the bread slices to make them flexible and with a 3-inch cookie cutter cut out bread rounds. Brush both sides of the rounds with melted butter or margarine and gently press the rounds into the cups of a 12-cup gem or small muffin tin. Bake the shells on the middle rack of the oven for 10 to 12 minutes, or until the edges are lightly browned. Let the shells cool in the tin for 5 minutes and turn them out on a rack to cool.

Toast cups can be frozen, wrapped in plastic wrap, for several months. To crisp them, arrange them on a baking sheet and heat them on the middle rack of a preheated 400-degree oven for 5 minutes. Fill them with Ham and Egg Butter, p. 16, Ratatouille, p. 91, scrambled eggs with chives, Curried Meat, p. 36, or Potted Shrimp, p. 43.

Rolling the bread first makes the rounds easier to press into place.

Finished toast cups can be gently stacked, wrapped in plastic wrap, and stored in the freezer for later use.

A snack of steaming soup on a frosty day.

CHAPTER TWO

Soups

Soup served with bowl and spoon may not seem snacklike, but a cup of hot soup on a cold winter day has become a snacking tradition. In summer, particularly when the weather is unbearably hot and humid, icy cold soup—you can even chill it with ice cubes—is marvelously refreshing.

Canned soups are unquestionably the fastest to prepare, but good as they are, they profit from a little doctoring up. Make your own additions according to individual preference. Give a lift to flavor with herbs and spices: oregano for vegetable soups, basil or curry powder for tomato-base soups, a soupçon of thyme added to pea soup. Avid soup drinkers might wish to keep fresh herbs, grown in pots in a sunny window, available year round. Chives and parsley are especially good sprinkled on soup after cooking. To make canned beef and chicken broth taste homemade, simmer 2 cups of broth with 2 tablespoons each of sliced onion, carrot, and celery, a sprig of parsley, and a pinch of thyme for about 20 minutes. Strain the broth, and you'd swear you made it from scratch. Chinese cooks adjust canned chicken broth to their taste by simmering 2 cups of broth for 10 minutes with a green onion and a slice of fresh ginger. Try it; while the broth simmers, soak a dried Chinese mushroom in hot water, then shred it and add it to the strained broth.

Soup snacks are among the best ways to use small amounts of leftovers. Rinse cooked vegetables under warm water to clean off any butter or sauce clinging to them, and cut small. Add them to the soup only at the last minute so they heat through, but don't cook further. The Basic Food Processor or Blender Soup uses leftover vegetables for quick cream soups, most of which can be enjoyed either hot or chilled. Leftover

19

noodles, rice, or pastas, provided they have not been mixed with sauce, can be added to any clear broth for a more substantial snack.

Each recipe in this chapter yields about two servings and can be easily doubled and even tripled.

Most homemade soups require a great deal of preparation and long cooking. Those that follow, however, are all easy, speedy, and brighter in flavor than their commercial cousins.

Consommé Bellevue
(Chicken and Clam Broth)

Simple though it is, this combination is extremely elegant.

> 2 cups chicken broth
> 1 cup clam juice
> 1 small clove garlic
> Cayenne to taste
> ½ teaspoon grated lemon rind
> 2 teaspoons finely chopped parsley

In a saucepan simmer the broth, clam juice, garlic, and cayenne for 15 minutes. Discard the garlic and serve the consommé in bowls garnished with lemon rind and parsley. Serves 2.

Harlequin Broth

> 2 cups beef broth or chicken broth
> ½ cup combined finely chopped fresh vegetables,
>   such as celery, green pepper, carrots, spinach,
>   watercress, parsley, green onions, or canned
>   water chestnuts
> 1 tablespoon finely chopped pimiento

In a saucepan simmer the vegetables in the beef or chicken broth until they are just tender. Serve the broth garnished with pimiento. Serves 1 to 2.

Food Processor or Blender Soup

Almost any vegetable—carrot, pea, tomato, cucumber, asparagus, broccoli, watercress—can be turned to soup in minutes. The basic recipe here is for a light cream soup, of delicate rather than zesty flavor.

If you have your choice of using either a food processor or a blender, the processor is preferable. It doesn't puree the vegetables to baby-food smoothness, but leaves a little "tooth." For the stock use canned chicken or beef broth, or soup cubes. Remember, however, that the cubes are salty, so if there is a lot of salt in the vegetables, it's better to stay with canned broth. Sautéed onion is important to the flavor. Including the onion, this soup takes very little time, and the result is worth the effort.

1 tablespoon butter or margarine
1 teaspoon vegetable oil
2 teaspoons finely chopped or grated onion
1 to 1½ cups leftover cooked vegetables
1½ cups beef broth or chicken broth, canned or made with soup cubes
¼ cup half-and-half or cream

In a saucepan sauté the onion in the butter or margarine and oil for 1 to 2 minutes. Remove the pan from the heat. In a food processor fitted with the metal blade or in a blender blend ½ cup beef or chicken broth and the vegetables to the desired texture. (If you want a smooth puree, add the sautéed onion as well.) Transfer the mixture to the saucepan, add the remaining broth, and bring it to a simmer. Add seasonings: pepper is basic, but consider such herbs as tarragon or dill, or a touch of curry powder. Simmer the soup for 1 minute and stir in the half-and-half or cream. Serve the soup hot.

Food Processor or Blender Gazpacho

If you like texture, reserve a little of the chopped green pepper and cucumber to float on top of this wonderful summer soup.

1 ripe tomato, peeled and cut into chunks, or ½ cup canned whole tomatoes (about 2), drained and crushed
½ cup peeled cucumber chunks
½ cup seeded chopped green pepper
¼ cup cold water
⅛ teaspoon salt
2 teaspoons red-wine vinegar
2 teaspoons olive oil
1 chopped green onion, including some of the green top
½ clove garlic

In a food processor fitted with the metal blade, or in a blender, puree all the ingredients. Pour the gazpacho into bowls and thoroughly chill it before serving, or quickly chill it by stirring in several ice cubes. Serves 1 to 2.

Curried Tomato Soup

¼ teaspoon curry powder
¼ teaspoon ground cumin
1 tablespoon butter or margarine
1 can tomato soup, diluted according to directions on the label
1 tomato, peeled, seeded, and coarsely chopped
Sour cream
2 teaspoons chopped chives

In a saucepan cook the curry powder and ground cumin in the butter or margarine for a few seconds to remove its raw taste. Add the diluted soup and the chopped tomato and bring the soup to a boil, stirring occasionally. Let the soup simmer for 1 minute, ladle it into bowls, and top each serving with a large spoonful of sour cream and a teaspoon of chives. Serves 2.

Turkish Treat
(Cucumber-Yogurt Soup)

1½ cups peeled grated cucumber
2 cups plain yogurt
2 teaspoons dried dill
2 tablespoons tarragon vinegar
Cayenne to taste
¼ cup chopped walnuts

In a bowl combine all the ingredients, except the nuts. Chill the soup. (Chill it quickly by adding ice cubes and serve them in the soup.) Sprinkle walnuts over each serving. Serves 2.

Hot fudge sundae served in a sherbet glass, garnished with whipped cream and slices of mandarin orange. (See p. 105.)

Three vegetarian snacks: cherry tomatoes sautéed in oil with garlic; mushrooms stuffed with hot-spiced cottage cheese; bean sprouts in a light Chinese dressing.

Sardines elegantly turned out as snack-sized canapés enlivened with a piquant sauce. (See p. 43.)

Sweet red peppers and tomatoes, golden summer squash, green zucchini, purple eggplant, chopped garlic and onion—the colorful and tasty makings of a Ratatouille. (See p. 91.)

Cold Curried Tomato Soup, topped with sour cream and chopped chives—from blender to bowl in minutes. (See p. 22.)

Garlic bread (p. 78) nestled among wedges of Date Bran Bread (p. 81),
Blueberry Muffins (p. 80), and jam-covered biscuits (p. 80), with quartered
pita pockets (p. 33) ready to be stuffed.

Beneath a Green Mayonnaise skin and lemon slice scales, the leftover half of a steamed bass. (See p. 44.)

Crudités—garden fresh vegetables served in a basket, the accompanying horseradish dip heaped into a sweet red pepper. (See p. 10.)

Four beautiful drinks: Orange Blush decorated with an orange wedge, Eggnog sprinkled with mace and bitter chocolate, Iced Coffee smothered in whipped cream and stirred with a cinnamon stick, a strawberry float with vanilla ice cream and a cherry. (See pp. 107–112.)

An earthy array of exotic flavors: Pie Crust Straws (p. 7) baked with cheese or sesame seeds, fried plantain slices (p. 5), Anchovy Toast (p. 7), Soy Chicken Wings (p. 27), Wheaten Cheese Crackers (p. 8), Keftedakia (tiny minty meatballs, p. 30), and, in the center, Potted Shrimp (p. 43).

Avgolemono Soup
(Greek Egg and Lemon Soup)

1½ to 2 cups chicken broth
3 tablespoons leftover rice (optional)
1 egg
1 tablespoon lemon juice, or to taste

In a saucepan bring the chicken broth to a slow simmer. In a mixing bowl beat the egg and lemon juice together. Add ¼ cup broth to the bowl, stirring, and slowly stir that mixture into the saucepan. Add the rice, if you are using it. Cook the soup for 1 minute or so until it is creamy. Do not let the soup boil or it will curdle. Serves 1 to 2.

Cheddar Cheese Soup

2 teaspoons butter or margarine
1 teaspoon vegetable oil
¼ cup chopped onion
¼ cup chopped celery
2 teaspoons flour
½ teaspoon dry mustard
1 cup chicken broth
1 cup milk
½ cup shredded cheddar cheese

In a saucepan sauté the onion and celery in the butter or margarine and oil for 3 to 5 minutes, or until the vegetables are softened. Do not let the onion brown. Blend in the flour and mustard and cook, stirring, for 2 minutes. Add the chicken broth and simmer about 5 minutes, or until the celery is tender. Add the milk, bring the soup to a simmer again, and stir in the cheese. Serve the soup as is, or blend it to the desired consistency in a food processor fitted with the metal blade, in a blender, or by hand by putting it through a food mill. Serves 2.

A munchy picnic snack of crisp Oven Fried Drumsticks.

CHAPTER THREE
Meat & Poultry

The easiest of all meat snacks are make-your-own deli combos that literally take the heat off the snacker. No cooking is involved, and little work other than setting out the meats, breads, condiments, and other accompaniments. The guests are involved, and the cold meat platter suits everyone (even card-carrying vegetarians, if you sneak in some cheeses). Dieters can nibble a bit of ham with a wisp of lettuce; those with heartier appetites can construct the legendary overstuffed sandwich—bulging with meat, cheese, lettuce, tomato, and any and everything else—known by a variety of names. To some it's a hero; to others a hoagy, a grinder, or a submarine. In New Orleans it's called a Po' Boy, a name that seems ironic since the traditional version of a Po' Boy also contains oysters, hardly an economy item these days.

In true melting-pot style Americans can choose from a splendid variety of cold meats re-created by waves of immigrants in their new homeland. Eastern European Jews introduced peppery pastrami, lean corned beef, and tongue. Germans brought liverwurst, smoked sausages, and headcheese. From Italy and Hungary came salami.

According to appetite, arrange a deli spread along strictly ethnic lines or happily mix selections, adding boiled ham, roast beef, and sliced turkey or chicken. Have a bevy of breads for the sandwich-builders: Jewish rye, pumpernickel, whole-grain, crusty Italian.

Condiments make the difference between a great deli snack and an ordinary one. Fortunately they are readily found in the supermarket, and once opened keep for a long time in the refrigerator. For the Jewish nosh, have sour and half-sour pickles, pickled green tomatoes, and fiery cherry peppers. For the mixed spread, go all out on the mustards: Dijon-type, hot deli-style, mild Düsseldorf, sweet mustard sauce, and mustard pickles. Put out chutney and horseradish to accompany roast beef, sweet watermelon pickle, and bread-and-butter pickles to accompany chicken or turkey.

If you want to go whole hog (and keep that vegetarian happy, too) include bottled roast peppers, artichoke hearts, olives, cherry tomatoes, lettuce leaves, or raw sauerkraut. No one will object if slices of provolone cheese and Swiss are on hand as well.

Few snacks are better than cold leftover meat, and the right condiment does more than assist—it ennobles. Some proven combinations: beef with mango chutney, pickled onions, or Italian mustard fruit; roast lamb with mint jelly, hot pepper jelly, or pickled watermelon rind; pork and poultry with mayonnaise, sweet pickle sauce, sweet mustard sauce, or cranberry jelly.

Many of the recipes that follow use leftover meats for casual picnic fare, as well as for hearty hashes, curries, and salads.

Oven-Fried Drumsticks

8 chicken drumsticks
¼ cup flour
½ teaspoon salt
1 teaspoon paprika
Pinch of cayenne (optional)
½ teaspoon dried thyme, pulverized
¼ cup butter or margarine, melted

Preheat the oven to 400 degrees. Rinse and dry the drumsticks with paper towels. In a paper bag large enough to hold the chicken, combine the flour, salt, paprika, and cayenne and add the drumsticks. Twist the top of the bag tightly and shake the bag to coat each drumstick evenly. Combine the butter or margarine with the thyme and with a pastry brush coat each drumstick with the mixture. Arrange the drumsticks in a single layer in a shallow baking pan, making sure they do not touch. Bake the drumsticks on the middle rack of the oven for 30 minutes, turn them, and coat them with the remaining butter mixture. Bake them for 15 minutes more, or until they are golden and tender when pierced with a fork. Serves 4 to 8.

Soy Chicken Wings

Cold fried chicken tends to get soggy, especially when packed for picnics. Soy wings, made without flour or fat, don't. The sugar glaze is only slightly sticky.

1 pound chicken wings (about 6 or 7 wings)
¼ cup soy sauce, preferably imported
¼ to ½ teaspoon ground ginger
2 teaspoons sugar
1 clove garlic, crushed

Rinse the wings, and cut off the wing tips. In a bowl combine the remaining ingredients and add the wings, letting them marinate in the refrigerator for 30 minutes or overnight. Turn them at least once. Preheat the oven to 350 degrees. In a baking pan or jelly-roll pan lined with foil, arrange the wings and bake them on the middle rack of the oven for 25 minutes. Turn them and bake them for 25 minutes more, or until they are nicely glazed and tender when pierced with a fork. Serve hot or cold. Serves 2.

Chopped Liver

1 large chicken liver, rinsed and cut in 4 pieces
1 tablespoon butter or margarine
1 teaspoon vegetable oil
1 shallot, finely chopped or grated, or 1 teaspoon finely chopped or grated onion or green onion
1 teaspoon Madeira, sherry, or brandy

Dry the liver pieces on paper towels. Heat the butter or margarine and oil in a small skillet until sizzling, add the liver pieces, and toss them over high heat until they are browned on all sides. Cut into a piece; it should be faintly pink on the inside. Remove the liver pieces to a chopping board and let them cool. Reduce the heat to medium, add the shallot; cook it, stirring, until it is soft and lightly browned. Remove the skillet from the heat. Chop the liver and transfer it to a plate. Add the Madeira to the pan, and heat it until it bubbles, scraping the bottom of the pan to loosen any residue. Pour the liquid over the liver, combine well, and spread the mixture on toast, or eat it as is. Serves 1.

Poultry Salad

A basic salad. Additions depend on what's on hand: chopped green onions or chives; diced celery; cucumber, peeled, seeded, and diced; chopped fresh dill or a judicious sprinkling of dried dill; curry powder to taste blended into the dressing; a pinch of thyme; half a tomato, peeled, seeded, and chopped; a teaspoon of chopped fresh basil, especially if you add the tomato. The possibilities are endless.

> *1 cup diced, skinless chicken, turkey, or duck*
> *¼ cup mayonnaise*
> *¼ cup sour cream*
> *1 teaspoon lemon juice or herb vinegar*

In a bowl combine the ingredients and toss to mix well. Serves 1.

Beef and Mushroom Salad

> *1 cup Vinaigrette, p. 84*
> *1 teaspoon Worcestershire sauce or imported soy sauce*
> *¼ cup chopped parsley*
> *2 tablespoons finely chopped green onion, including some of the green tops, or shallots*
> *½ pound mushrooms, wiped with a damp towel and thinly sliced*
> *1½ to 2 cups thinly sliced strips of cooked steak, roast beef, or pot roast*
> *Salt and pepper to taste*
> *4 cups torn salad greens, washed and chilled*

In a salad bowl combine the basic Vinaigrette, Worcestershire sauce or soy sauce, parsley, and green onion, add the mushrooms and meat strips, and toss to coat them with the dressing. Add salt and pepper to taste. Let the mixture marinate for 30 minutes at room temperature or overnight in the refrigerator. Let the salad return to room temperature before serving. Toss in the chilled greens just before serving. Serves 2 to 4.

Teriyaki Strips

Use any boneless cut of beef, such as round or top sirloin, or pork, such as boned loin or shoulder, for this recipe. If you're doubling this recipe, fry the meat in two batches, then return all the meat to the pan and finish cooking in the sauce. More than ½ cup meat lowers the temperature of the oil, so that the meat steams rather than fries. If you have no wok, use a heavy skillet, and toss the meat with a spatula.

> *½ cup very thin meat strips, cut 2 by 1 inches*
> *1 tablespoon teriyaki sauce*
> *1 tablespoon vegetable oil, preferably peanut*

Sauce

> *¼ cup chicken broth or water*
> *½ teaspoon cornstarch*
> *1 teaspoon teriyaki sauce*

In a bowl let the meat marinate in the teriyaki sauce for 5 minutes and drain it. Heat the oil in a wok or skillet to sizzling, add the meat, and stir-fry or toss it, keeping it in motion so that the strips brown evenly. Cook beef for 2 to 3 minutes; pork for 3 to 4. (Pork must be thoroughly cooked. It will turn a lighter color when done.)

In a small bowl combine all the ingredients for the sauce, stirring well to dissolve the cornstarch. Just before the end of the cooking time for the meat, restir the mixture and pour it over the meat in the wok and simmer, covered, for 1 to 2 minutes, or until the sauce thickens slightly. Serves 1.

Ultimate Hamburger

Very lean beef, that with less than 22 percent fat, produces dry burgers. Beef with somewhat more fat produces juicier, more flavorful ones. Use your judgment, depending on your taste and your diet.

1 pound lean ground beef
¼ teaspoon salt
*¼ cup mayonnaise stirred with 2 tablespoons
     catsup and 1 tablespoon sweet pickle relish*
3 hamburger buns, split and toasted
3 thick tomato slices
3 thin sweet onion slices
Dill pickle spears (optional)

Shape the beef into 3 thick patties, handling the meat as
little as possible. (If the patties are too compact, prick them
all over with a fork.) Heat a skillet over medium-high heat
until a drop of water beads on the surface. Sprinkle the salt
in the skillet and grill the patties for 3 minutes on each side,
or until done as desired. Divide the mayonnaise mixture
among the buns, top three buns with a patty apiece, a slice of
tomato and onion, and the remaining bun. Serve with pickles,
if desired. Serves 3.

Keftedakia
(Cold Minted Meatballs)

In Greece these tiny meatballs are served at room temperature as part of an appetizer tray. Ouzo, an anise flavored
aperitif, lends a distinctive flavor, but wine or water may be
used instead. They make perfect picnic fare, too. Carry them
in plastic ice-cube trays or empty plastic egg cartons.

1 cup fresh white bread crumbs
¼ cup ouzo, dry white wine, or water
5 tablespoons olive oil
½ cup finely chopped or grated onion
1 pound lean ground beef or lamb
1 egg
*1 tablespoon chopped fresh mint, or 1 teaspoon
     crumbled dried mint*
1 clove garlic, minced
½ teaspoon crumbled oregano
1 teaspoon salt
Freshly ground pepper to taste
Flour

In a bowl soak the bread crumbs in the ouzo or wine. In a heavy skillet sauté the onion in the oil until it is translucent, and transfer it with a slotted spoon to a deep bowl. Squeeze out the bread crumbs, discarding the liquid. Knead together until thoroughly blended the bread crumbs, onion, beef or lamb, egg, mint, garlic, oregano, salt, and pepper to taste. Form 1-inch balls, roll them evenly in flour, and refrigerate them for about 1 hour. (This allows the flour to dry, ensuring a crisp crust.) Reheat the oil in the skillet to very hot and sizzling, adding more oil if necessary, and fry the meatballs, about 8 at a time, turning them frequently, until crisp and brown on all sides. Drain them on paper towels and serve them chilled. Makes about 30.

Steak Tartare

Because it is ill-advised to let raw ground beef stand unrefrigerated for any length of time at all, this recipe must be prepared at the last minute. A little extra trouble, but well worth the effort.

> *½ pound boneless beef, such as tenderloin or top*
>   *round, trimmed*
> *2 raw egg yolks*
> *2 tablespoons finely chopped or grated onion*
> *2 tablespoons capers, drained*
> *2 tablespoons chopped parsley*
> *Salt and freshly ground pepper to taste*
> *Pumpernickel or rye bread, buttered*

In a food processor fitted with the metal blade, or in a meat grinder, finely grind the beef. Mound it on a platter, making a well in the center in which to put the egg yolks. Arrange the onion, capers, and parsley around the side of the platter, combine the ingredients, add salt and pepper to taste. Serve with dark bread and condiments such as Dijon-type mustard, Worcestershire sauce, or hot-pepper sauce.

Pita Stuffers

Hot or cold, eaten indoors or on a picnic, made with leftover ground meat or fresh patties, a stuffed pita pocket is a filling, nourishing, spicy snack. If working in a kitchen, cut off the tops of pita pockets, warm them briefly in the oven, and serve them and the stuffing separately so people can help themselves. For a picnic, stuff each pocket ahead of time and slip it open end up into a plastic bag. Gather the top of the bag tightly around the stuffed pita, twist it, and secure it with a small rubber band. The pita bread will hold up a lot better than sandwiches do, even after the rigors of a long journey in hot weather.

Dilled Hamburger Pita

1 hamburger patty
Salt and pepper to taste
1 tablespoon chopped fresh dill, or ½ teaspoon
*   dried dill*
1 slice Muenster or mozzarella cheese
Shredded lettuce

Broil or pan-fry the hamburger to taste, season it with salt, pepper, and dill, and insert it, the cheese, and lettuce shreds into the pita pocket. Eat as is, or warm it on a baking sheet in a low oven until the cheese melts. Serves 1.

Chili Pitas

½ pound ground beef
2 teaspoons chili powder
Salt and pepper to taste
2 teaspoons vegetable oil
2 tablespoons catsup or chili sauce
2 or 3 slices Monterey Jack cheese

Season the beef with chili powder, salt, and pepper and in a skillet brown it in the oil. Drain off the fat from the skillet and stir in the catsup or chili sauce. Stuff the meat into pita pockets, adding a slice of cheese to each. Serves 2 or 3.

Vegetarian Pitas

⅓ cup bean sprouts, fresh or canned
⅓ cup combined raw chopped vegetables, such
*   as green pepper, carrot, mushrooms, radishes,*
*   celery*
2 tablespoons Blue Cheese Dressing, p. 84, or to
*   taste*

In a bowl combine all the ingredients and stuff the mixture into pita pockets. Makes 2.

Meat Hash

For the perfect hash you need freshly boiled potatoes. It needn't take long: peeled potato, cut into ¼-inch cubes, parboils in about 10 minutes.

> 2 tablespoons butter or margarine
> 1 tablespoon vegetable oil
> 3 tablespoons chopped onion
> 1 tablespoon chopped seeded green pepper or celery
> 1 cup cubed parboiled potatoes
> 1 cup finely chopped cooked beef, corned beef, lamb, or ham
> Salt and pepper to taste
> Dash of Worcestershire sauce (for beef or lamb only)

In an 8-inch skillet heat the butter or margarine and oil until sizzling, and sauté the onion and pepper or celery for 3 to 5 minutes until they soften. Reduce the heat to medium, add the potatoes and meat, and season the hash with salt, pepper, and Worcestershire sauce. Pat the hash down with a pancake turner, and cook for 5 to 7 minutes or until bits of crust form on the bottom. Drain off any excess fat before serving. Serves 2 or 3.

Poultry Hash

In a saucepan heat cubed cooked chicken or turkey and cubed parboiled potato or chopped celery in leftover gravy or sauce. Season the mixture with salt and pepper and add chopped chives, parsley, thyme, or marjoram to taste. The rule of thumb for measurements is half as much gravy as other ingredients. Thus, for ½ cup of poultry and ½ cup of potatoes, you will need ½ cup of gravy or sauce. Heat the hash thoroughly, but do not overcook it.

New Shapes for Sandwich Meats

The pleasure of a snack can be as much in how it looks as how it tastes. These ideas combine unique flavor with interesting shapes—and they can all be eaten with hands. Horseradish Salami Rolls and Dried Beef and Canteloupe on Picks are classy enough for a cocktail party. Bologna Pie is a favorite of the preschool crowd.

Bologna Pie: Spread cream cheese with chives on Lebanon bologna, summer sausage, or mortadella. Top with another slice of the luncheon meat, spread again with cheese. Keep layering until the "pie" is about an inch high. Cut into wedges.

Horseradish Salami Rolls: Season whipped cream with horseradish to taste, put one teaspoonful on a thin slice of hard salami, roll, and secure with a toothpick.

Deli Kabobs: Make kababs on toothpicks of small cubes of ham and cheese; add an olive or a tiny gherkin. Serve with a dip of mustard, seasoned to taste with honey and lemon juice.

Dried Beef and Canteloupe on Picks: Quarter a ripe canteloupe and scoop out the seeds. Open a jar of dried beef and separate the slices. Use a melon baller to scoop out balls, or cut the melon into small squares. Fold a 2-inch square of beef into a small package, and spear first the beef, then the melon balls, on toothpicks.

No matter how humble the ingredients, spearing meats and cheeses on a toothpick turns them into a delicacy. Try Deli Kabobs on meal-bored children, or serve them as card party snacks.

Creamed Meat or Poultry

Depending on the meat or poultry that is left over and your own fancy, season this dish with thyme, paprika, tarragon, or a little sweet pickle relish. Making the sauce should take no more than 6 or 7 minutes.

1 tablespoon butter or margarine
1 tablespoon flour
¾ cup milk, or a combination of milk and
*   chicken broth*
½ to 1 cup chopped cooked veal, ham, turkey, or
*   chicken*
Salt and pepper to taste
Herbs or seasoning to taste
2 teaspoons dry sherry (optional)
1 tablespoon chopped parsley

In a medium-size saucepan melt the butter or margarine over moderate heat and stir in the flour. Cook the mixture, stirring, for 1 minute until it is blended, and add the milk or broth. Stir the mixture until it thickens. Lower the heat and simmer the sauce for a few minutes to remove the "raw" taste of flour. Stir in the meat or poultry and add salt, pepper, and other seasonings to taste. Simmer until the mixture is thoroughly heated. Just before serving, stir in the sherry, transfer the mixture to a plate, and sprinkle it with parsley. Serves 2.

Curried Meat or Poultry

Some like it hot, some mild, so it's difficult to specify how much curry powder to use. Also, different brands vary in strength. Furthermore, curry powder that has been opened and sitting in the cupboard for several months will have lost much of its zap. At any rate, adding ground cumin deepens the curry flavor. It is important to cook the two powders in oil or fat for a short time, to remove the "raw" taste.

¼ cup chopped onion
2 tablespoons vegetable oil, butter, or margarine
2 teaspoons curry powder, or to taste
1 teaspoon ground cumin
¾ cup chicken broth, tomato juice, or water
¼ cup combined diced fresh and dried fruit,
*   such as apples, peaches, or dried currants or*
*   raisins*

*½ cup chopped vegetables, raw or cooked, such
     as carrots, radishes, green peppers, cauli-
     flower*
*½ to 1 cup cubed cooked beef, pork, lamb, or
     poultry*
Salt to taste
*1 teaspoon cornstarch, dissolved in 1 tablespoon
     cold water (optional)*
2 tablespoons cream or half-and-half (optional)

In a medium-size saucepan sauté the onion over high heat
in the oil, butter, or margarine for a few minutes, stirring,
until it begins to brown. Add the curry powder and ground
cumin, and cook the mixture for 1 minute more, stirring. Add
the liquid, the fruit, and any raw vegetables, cover the pan,
and cook the mixture over medium heat until the vegetables
are tender. Stir, add any cooked vegetables, the meat or poultry, and salt to taste. Cook until all the ingredients are thoroughly heated. If you want a thickened sauce, bring the
mixture to the boil and stir in the cornstarch mixture. For a
smoother, milder sauce stir in the cream or half-and-half off
the heat. Serve the curry with such accompaniments as sliced
banana in yogurt, chopped peanuts, chopped tomatoes, or popadums. Serves 2.

Poached Marrow

If you are on friendly terms with your meat man, he'll probably give you marrow bones for free. Ask him to saw the
bones into 2-inch sections. If you must buy the bones in larger
pieces as they are sold for making soup, you will still be able
to get the marrow out by using an iced-tea spoon instead of a
knife.

*3 pounds beef marrow bones, preferably cut into
     2-inch sections*
Salt and pepper to taste
Bread or toast

With a paring knife, remove the marrow from sections of
bone, or scoop the marrow out with a spoon from larger

pieces of bone. Cut the marrow into ¼-inch-thick slices. In a saucepan, bring an inch of salted water to a boil. Lower the flame so the water barely simmers, and poach the marrow slices, a few at a time, for about 2 minutes. Remove them with a slotted spoon and drain on paper towels. Spread the marrow while still warm on bread or toast, and sprinkle with salt and pepper. Serves 2 to 4.

Cold marrow can be removed from a short section of bone all in one piece and sliced neatly for poaching. Or poach the bones with the marrow still inside in salted water to cover. Remove the bones, and when they are cool enough to handle scoop the cooked marrow out with an iced tea spoon or with a small knife.

The Sophisticated Snacker

The international snacks here are Soy Chicken Wings, Keftedakia, Pie Crust Straws, Anchovy Toast, and Potted Shrimp.

Try seasoning that quintessential American institution, the cocktail party, with international flavor. Serve a buffet of snack foods drawn from around the world. You might hesitate to spring new and unusual foods on dinner guests, but since at a buffet, people can sample foods as they choose or not, this is the occasion to introduce your friends to foreign appetizers that will delight the majority, and may even tempt those with timid palates.

It's surprising how an array of snacks drawn from very different cultures can complement one another. Everyone abandons the precepts of a formal meal and finds that Keftedakia, cool and minty, accord very well with a Chinese Soy Wing and a few Caribbean Plantain Chips. Plan your menu around one or two meat dishes, consider a seafood too, and then add vegetable dishes and crisp tidbits for variety. A sample buffet might be:

Soy Chicken Wings (Chinese)
Keftedakia (Greek)
Potted Shrimp (English)
Plantain Chips (Caribbean)
Crudités (French) and Sour Cream Dip
Tabbouleh (Middle Eastern)

A cold fish with Green Mayonnaise for the discriminating midnight snacker.

CHAPTER FOUR
Fish

For impromptu snacks that are elegant, subtle, and no work at all, invest in a few prepared fish delicacies. Serve smoked mussels or oysters out of the opened tin, with toothpicks to winkle them out. Surround a small jar of red or black lumpfish caviar or salmon roe with chopped onion, chopped hard-boiled eggs, lemon wedges, and Melba toast rounds or crackers. Either roe is also good with a spoonful of sour cream on an artichoke heart. Experiment with sardines in sauce: tomato and port wine; curry; mustard and Worcestershire. Or serve them cold in sour cream sprinkled with seasoned salt, or mashed with sieved hard-boiled egg, lemon juice, and Worcestershire sauce. Herring tidbits, which some find too sweet, can be modified by pouring off some of the sauce and diluting the rest with sour cream.

People lucky enough to have a good deli department or a Jewish delicatessen to buy from should not be afraid to try various smoked fish, such as whitefish or chubb. They are not particularly "fishy" in flavor, and the best-quality smoked fish is not oversalted either. The traditional Jewish fish snack is one or an assortment of smoked fish, served with split toasted bagels and generous quantities of cream cheese.

With cans of tuna, sardines, shrimp, clams, and oysters in the pantry, you have the essentials for making a raft of briny treats, for company or just for yourself. The trick of turning seafood into classic snacks is barely more difficult than the casual suggestions above. The recipes here don't call for fresh seafood because most people are unlikely to have a handful of raw shrimp around. But should that rare event occur, feel free to substitute fresh for canned or bottled shellfish.

41

Italian Tuna Salad

This salad contains most of the ingredients used in the sauce that accompanies cold veal in the classic Italian dish called Vitello Tonnato.

1 6½-ounce can chunk tuna
3 to 4 tablespoons mayonnaise
2 flat anchovy filets, drained and finely chopped
1 tablespoon chopped green onion, including some of the green top
2 tablespoons capers, drained
2 tablespoons lemon juice
Salt and pepper to taste

Drain the tuna, flake it with a fork into a bowl, and combine it with mayonnaise. (Water-packed tuna may need more mayonnaise than oil-packed.) Fold in the anchovy, green onion, capers, and lemon juice and gently turn the mixture to combine it. Add salt and pepper to taste. Serve the salad as is, or on a bed of lettuce. Serves 2.

Herbed Tuna Salad

1 6½-ounce can chunk tuna, preferably white
3 tablespoons Vinaigrette, p. 84
½ teaspoon dried thyme, pulverized
1 tablespoon chopped green onion, including some of the green top
Chopped fresh raw vegetables, such as green pepper, celery, cucumber, or carrots, up to ½ cup
Salt and pepper to taste
Chopped parsley

Drain the tuna and flake it with a fork into a bowl. Add the basic Vinaigrette, thyme, and the vegetables, folding them in gently. Add salt and pepper to taste and before serving garnish the salad with chopped parsley. Serves 2.

Curried Tuna Salad

1 6½-ounce can chunk tuna, preferably white
1 teaspoon curry powder
¼ cup sour cream
Chopped green pepper and/or raw cauliflower
*   flowerets, up to ½ cup*
Salt and pepper to taste

Drain and flake the tuna with a fork into a bowl. Mix the curry powder into the sour cream, and add to the tuna. Add the vegetables, folding them in gently. Add salt and pepper to taste. Serves 2.

Sardine Canapé

1 tablespoon butter or margarine
¼ cup chopped onion
2 tablespoons catsup
2 tablespoons dry white wine or white vermouth
1 teaspoon Worcestershire sauce
1 can (4⅜ oz. or 3¾ oz.) sardines,
*   drained*

In a skillet sauté the onion in the butter or margarine until it is translucent. Add the catsup, white wine or vermouth, and Worcestershire sauce and bring to a simmer. Add the sardines, being careful not to break them. Turn them once to heat through. Serve the sardines on toast rounds, or build a fancier canapé by placing a slice of tomato on the toast round, then the sardines and sauce, and top it off with a slice of hard-boiled egg and a sprig of watercress. Serves 2.

Potted Shrimp

Potted shrimp have been an English tea party standby since Edwardian days. Today they're a big hit at cocktail time. The canned shrimp used in this version are simply mixed with the other ingredients, as they require no further cooking. With a clarified butter seal they will keep for several days in the refrigerator.

½ cup plus 3 tablespoons butter
¼ teaspoon ground nutmeg
Cayenne
¼ teaspoon salt, or to taste
1 cup tiny canned shrimp, drained in a sieve
  and rinsed under cold running water

In a small heavy saucepan slowly melt 3 tablespoons of butter and skim off the froth on the surface. Let the butter stand or settle off the heat for a minute and spoon it into a pouring cup, being careful not to include any of the white solids on the bottom of the pan. Discard the solids. In a larger saucepan or a skillet melt the remaining butter and stir in the nutmeg, a sprinkle of cayenne, salt, and shrimp. Turn the shrimp to coat them with the butter mixture and divide them equally among 3 or 4 jars, custard cups, or other small containers. Seal the containers by pouring a thin layer of clarified butter over the surface. Serve potted shrimp spread on toast or crackers.

Seafood Sauces

These are three classic sauces for cold seafood: Green Mayonnaise, Cocktail Sauce, and Tartar Sauce. You may associate cocktail sauce with shrimp cocktail, but it is every bit as good with clams, oysters, or crab meat. Serve either green mayonnaise or tartar sauce with leftover cold fish. Or flake the fish and mix it gently with the sauce to create a fish salad. Add chopped cucumber or diced celery for crunchiness. Fish salad looks elegant heaped into a lettuce leaf, but tastes even better on slices of rye toast.

Green Mayonnaise
To ½ cup mayonnaise add ¼ cup very finely chopped fresh herbs, such as watercress, parsley, spinach leaves, chives, and tarragon. Mix well. Makes ½ cup.

Cocktail Sauce
½ cup chili sauce
1 teaspoon Worcestershire sauce
½ teaspoon dry mustard
1 teaspoon prepared horseradish
1 teaspoon lemon juice

Dash of hot-pepper sauce
Salt and pepper to taste

Blend all the ingredients well. Makes ½ cup.

Tartar Sauce
½ cup mayonnaise
½ teaspoon spicy brown mustard
2 teaspoons finely chopped sweet pickle
½ teaspoon capers, drained
1 teaspoon lemon juice
1 teaspoon finely chopped chives or onion

Combine all the ingredients and mix them carefully to avoid crushing the capers. Makes ½ cup.

Clam Hash

> *2 cups cold, diced boiled potatoes*
> *½ cup chopped onion*
> *¼ teaspoon dried thyme, pulverized*
> *1 6-ounce can clams, partially drained*
> *2 tablespoons bacon fat, butter, or margarine*
> *Salt and pepper to taste*
> *2 strips crisp cooked bacon, crumbled*

In a bowl let the potatoes, onion, thyme, and clams with some of their liquid stand at room temperature for 10 to 20 minutes so that the potatoes absorb the liquid. In a heavy skillet heat the bacon fat, butter, or margarine, add the clam mixture, and cook it slowly, stirring occasionally, until the potatoes are lightly browned. Add salt and pepper to taste and sprinkle the crumbled bacon over the hash. Serves 2.

Oyster Stew

Nothing could be quicker or easier—or more delicious and warming.

> *1 8-ounce can oysters with their liquor*
> *1 cup half-and-half*
> *1 tablespoon butter or margarine*
> *Dash of Worcestershire sauce (optional)*
> *Cayenne or paprika*

In a small saucepan heat the oysters and their liquor and the half-and-half over medium heat until the mixture bubbles. Add the butter or margarine and let the stew simmer for a few minutes until the oysters are heated and plumped. Add the seasonings to taste. Serve the stew with oyster crackers or water biscuits. Serves 2.

Cheese Fondue, fondly shared by an open fire.

CHAPTER FIVE
Cheese & Eggs

At any season, for any occasion, an array of cheeses makes a splendid snack. A cheese tray suits a late-night poker session, a casual gathering of friends, an elegant cocktail party. The number of choices needn't be large—as few as three offerings will keep a small group munching happily—but the cheeses should be varied in texture and flavor. As a rule of thumb, include one or two popular favorites such as a mellow cheddar or a perfectly ripened Brie or Camembert, and introduce a small wedge of smoked Gouda or Port du Salut, or any cheese that may be new to you or your guests. Suit the cheese to the drinks served; Limburger is terrific with beer but not with white wine. Let cheese come to room temperature and set it out with baskets of crackers and crunchy French or Italian bread, and plenty of knives and a cheese-parer.

With the addition of fruit—ripe, juicy pears and chilled green grapes in particular—such a snack serves easily as a whole lunch or an impromptu dessert.

The easiest way to categorize cheese is by degree of hardness. Selections in each category are listed below.

> *Hard: Cheddar, Swiss, Emmenthaler, Gruyère, Cheshire, Provolone, Sage, Gouda, Edam, Coon, Kasseri*
> *Semi-Soft: Bel Paese, Cantal, Feta, Fontina, Limburger, Monterey Jack, Mozzarella, Muenster, Pont l'Eveque, Port du Salut, Tilset*
> *Semi-Soft Blue-Veined: Roquefort, Danish Blue, Blue, Gorgonzola, Stilton*

> *Soft: Brie, Camembret, Neufchatel,*
>   *Liederkranz*
> *Soft Cream-Type: Crema Danica, Creme*
>   *Chantilly, Petit Suisse, Cream Cheese*

Both the cheese and egg dishes here range all the way from a cottage cheese snack on the run, to the meal-sized—but snack-quick—Egg Fu Yung. Double, or even quadruple the recipes for Cheese Fondue and Welsh Rarebit to provide snacks for a crowd.

Cottage Cheese Variations

Cottage cheese alone is healthful, filling, low in calories—and bland. But because it has little character of its own, it "marries" well with a variety of flavorings. A half-cup portion makes an adequate snack for one. Use either small- or large-curd cottage cheese, according to your preference.

Cottage Cheese and Sour Cream

Mix 2 tablespoons sour cream into ½ cup cottage cheese. It adds calories, alas, but makes the cheese delightfully creamy.

Garden Cottage Cheese

Mix ¼ cup coarsely chopped or finely grated raw vegetables into ½ cup cottage cheese. Some suggestions, alone or in combination: cabbage, carrots, celery, cucumber, chives, mushrooms, radishes, fennel, tomato, parsley, green onions, green or red peppers, watercress. Also drained canned water chestnuts, hearts of palm, and beets. Season with salt and pepper to taste.

Cottage Cheese with Horseradish

Mix prepared horseradish to taste into ½ cup cottage cheese. Add a dash of Worcestershire sauce.

Cottage Cheese with Black Pepper

Add a liberal quantity of coarse black pepper, preferably freshly ground, to ½ cup cottage cheese.

Cottage Cheese with Diced Fruit

Mix ½ cup diced fresh or drained water-packed fruit into ½ cup cottage cheese. Some suggestions, alone or in combination: melons, berries, mandarin orange sections, apples, pineapple, peaches, apricots, seedless grapes, kiwi, mangoes, papayas, bananas.

Cheese Fondue

2 slices firm-textured bread, crusts trimmed and cut into ¼-inch cubes
2¾ cups (about ¾ pound) shredded sharp cheddar cheese
¾ cup milk
1 teaspoon dry mustard
¼ teaspoon salt
Cayenne
1 egg, lightly beaten
1 tablespoon butter or margarine
6 slices toast, cut into squares
Paprika

In the top of a double boiler combine the bread cubes, cheese, milk, mustard, salt, and cayenne to taste over hot water, and stir constantly until the cheese is melted and the mixture is thickened. Beat in the egg and butter or margarine and cook, stirring, for 5 minutes more. Transfer the fondue to a serving bowl, sprinkle it with paprika, and serve it as a dipping sauce with toast squares. Serves 3 to 6.

Welsh Rarebit

2 cups shredded cheddar cheese
1 tablespoon flour
¼ cup beer
1 tablespoon butter or margarine
1 teaspoon Worcestershire sauce, or to taste
¼ teaspoon dry mustard
Cayenne
2 toast slices or 4 grilled tomato slices

In a bowl toss the cheese with the flour. (Flour allows the cheese to melt evenly without becoming gluey.) In a heavy saucepan combine the floured cheese, beer, butter or margarine, Worcestershire sauce, mustard, and cayenne to taste over moderate heat, stirring constantly to blend. Do not let the mixture boil. Arrange toast slices or grilled tomato slices in a shallow ovenproof dish and cover with the rarebit. Broil the rarebit for 1 to 2 minutes, or until the top is brown. Serve at once. Serves 2.

Spiedini
(Italian Baked Cheese Loaf)

Spiedini is utter bliss—but bliss has its price. The caloric count is probably over a googol, which in mathematical jargon means the number 1 followed by 100 zeros. If you're taking the plunge, use butter and the best French or Italian bread you can find. The anchovies give a necessary piquancy to this dish—even confirmed anchovy avoiders like them with spiedini.

1 loaf French or Italian bread
1 8-ounce package mozzarella cheese, cut into ½-
*   inch slices*
4 anchovy fillets, or to taste, drained
4 tablespoons butter or margarine

Preheat the oven to 500 degrees. With a serrated knife trim the ends, sides, and top from the loaf, leaving the bottom crust on. You now have a squared-off rectangle. Cut it in half. In each half make cuts, about an inch apart, cutting down to—but not through—the crust. Trim the slices of mozzarella

Long Day, Light Supper

No need to belabor the obvious: when you come home late and tired, you don't want to take the time and energy to prepare a full meal. Yet to stand in front of the refrigerator pawing around for a little of this and a little of that is not a cheerful ending to a hard day. This is the time for a snack supper, one that appeals to the aesthetic as well as the gustatory tastes.

With minimal effort you can use an egg or cheese dish as the focus of a rounded meal of balanced tastes and textures; the combinations below are examples of quick and satisfying small repasts. If your appetite calls for more, begin with a slightly elegant touch that needs no preparation, such as a few olives or smoked oysters. If you want dessert, ice cream or candy make for a sweet ending to supper.

Here are four menus as examples, all taken from recipes in this book.

Easy Omelet
Sautéed Cherry Tomatoes
Garlic Bread

Cheese Fondue
Onion, Orange, and Olive Salad

Curried Tomato Soup
Stuffed Eggs
Bean Sprout Salad

One-Eyed Texan
Garden Cottage Cheese

to fit into the cuts and place them in the cuts. Run long skewers lengthwise through the bread halves to hold the cheese in place. Put the bread halves in a shallow baking dish and arrange the anchovies on top. Melt the butter or margarine and pour it over the spiedini, moistening them evenly. Bake the bread on the middle rack of the oven for 8 to 10 minutes, using a bulb baster to draw up the butter in the pan and baste the spiedini several times, until the cheese is melted and the bread is crisp and golden. Eat with knives and forks. Serves 2 to 4.

Frittatas
(Italian Omelets)

Frittatas are flat omelets browned on both sides. They're a wonderful way to use up leftover cooked vegetables and meats, and they are good warm or at room temperature. Cut them into wedges or squares for cocktail snacks or picnic fare, and top with a dab of yogurt or sour cream. For ease in flipping a frittata, use a heavy 8-inch nonstick skillet.

1 tablespoon butter or margarine
1 teaspoon vegetable oil
½ cup combined chopped cooked or fresh vegetables, such as green onion or onion, green or red peppers, tomato, zucchini, cauliflower, or parsley
3 eggs, lightly beaten
¼ teaspoon oregano, pulverized
1 tablespoon grated Parmesan or Romano cheese
⅛ teaspoon salt

In an 8-inch skillet sauté fresh vegetables in the butter or margarine and oil until they are cooked but still crisp, or reheat leftover vegetables. To the beaten eggs add the oregano, cheese, and salt and combine. Spread the vegetables in the skillet, slowly pour the egg mixture over them, and cover the skillet. Cook the frittata over very low heat for about 7 minutes, or until the edges are firm but the center is still moist. Flip the frittata and brown the other side, uncovered, just long enough to set. Slide the frittata out onto a plate and serve.

Stuffed Eggs

Stuffed eggs are rather like peanuts, in that people can seldom restrain themselves enough to eat just one!

To keep eggs from cracking as they boil—or, more properly, simmer—pierce the large end with an egg pricker or a pin. Put the eggs in a saucepan with enough water to cover them by an inch, bring the water to a boil, and lower the heat to a gentle simmer. Add 1½ teaspoons of salt for each quart of water. (Salt makes the peeling easier.) Refrigerated large eggs cook in 12 minutes; for small eggs subtract 1 minute; for extra-large eggs, add 1 minute. When cooked, plunge the eggs into cold water, let them cool, and peel them under cold running water. Place the eggs in a bowl of cold water until you are ready to stuff them.

Seasoning the yolks is a matter of taste, both as to texture and flavor. Those who prefer a more solid result should go easy with the mayonnaise or sour cream; those who like a soft mixture can be more generous. As a general rule, 1 teaspoon of mayonnaise or sour cream per egg yolk is sufficient. Slice the eggs in half lengthwise, remove the yolks, and place them in a mixing bowl. With a fork, mash the yolks, mix them with mayonnaise or sour cream, and season them with salt and pepper. A variety of other seasonings, all to taste, follows:

Deviled Eggs: Add to the seasoned yolks a dash of Worcestershire sauce, a few drops of hot-pepper sauce, a little dry mustard, lemon juice, and paprika to color. If desired, add diced sweet pickle.

Gingered Eggs: Beat softened cream cheese and chopped candied ginger into sour cream–seasoned yolks.

Salmon Eggs: Add to the seasoned yolks drained and flaked canned salmon and a little grated onion. Top each stuffed half with a large caper or several small ones.

Herbed Eggs: Into the seasoned yolks stir finely chopped fresh herbs, such as tarragon, parsley, basil, or chervil.

Curried Eggs: Add to the seasoned yolks curry powder and fold in chopped chutney.

Ham and Eggs: Stuff the eggs with Ham and Egg Butter, p. 16. Reserve the extra yolks to rice or sieve as a topping for green salads.

Potato Frittata

In the master recipe substitute ½ cup sliced fried leftover boiled potatoes for the vegetables. Omit the cheese and oregano.

Hearty Frittata

In the master recipe substitute ¼ cup cubed leftover cooked ham or steak, reheated, for ¼ cup of the vegetables.

The Easy Omelet

How the French omelet ever earned its reputation for difficulty is a culinary mystery. Perhaps if it had been called the Easy Omelet, the problem would never have arisen. Time is the only enemy of the tender omelet; the quicker it cooks, the creamier and lighter it will be. Don't be tempted to use more than two eggs—the result will be heavy, and with a little practice you can make three to four individual omelets in less time than it takes to boil an egg. For best results use a heavy nonstick 8-inch skillet.

> 2 eggs
> 1/8 teaspoon salt
> 1 1/2 tablespoons butter or margarine

Break the eggs into a small bowl, add the salt, and beat for about 30 strokes with a fork to blend the yolks and whites; do not beat to the frothy stage or the omelet will be tough. Melt the butter or margarine over medium-high heat, tilting the skillet so that all surfaces are coated. The butter or margarine is the correct heat to cook the omelet when the foam has subsided. Pour the eggs into the skillet all at once, spreading them with the flat of a fork. When the mixture has "set" but the center is still runny, add a filling, and roll the omelet onto a plate. There is no limit to what sort of filling or seasoning you can use. Cooked spinach, seasoned with pepper and a pinch of nutmeg, is delicious. Finely chopped boiled ham, Westphalian ham, or prosciutto are good, too. So is crumbled cooked bacon. Chopped leftover cooked chicken or turkey makes a more interesting filling if combined with sautéed chopped onion and a sprinkling of tarragon. Kids appreciate the simplest filling of all—a tablespoon of currant jelly. And here are some other ideas:

Herbed Omelet: Add 1 tablespoon chopped fresh herbs to the beaten eggs; chives, basil, tarragon, parsley, chervil, or dill.

Cheese Omelet: Sprinkle 2 tablespoons shredded cheddar, Swiss, or Gruyère cheese or 1 tablespoon crumbled blue cheese over the omelet just before folding it.

Cottage Cheese and Chive Omelet: Spread 2 tablespoons cottage cheese mixed with chives over the upper half of the omelet just before rolling it.

Chutney and Sour Cream Omelet: Mix 1 tablespoon chopped chutney into 1 tablespoon sour cream. Spread it over the upper half of the omelet just before rolling it.

When the butter froth has subsided, pour the eggs into the skillet. The skillet should be hot enough so that the eggs sizzle.

With the flat of a fork, quickly spread the eggs evenly around the skillet in a circular motion.

When the omelet has set but the center is still slightly runny, add a filling.

Grasp the skillet, fingers up, and tilt it over a plate. Beginning near the handle, with the side of a fork gently push and roll the omelet forward onto the plate.

Crab or Shrimp Fu Yung

Called "pancakes," these are really fried omelets.

> *1 7-ounce can of crab meat or tiny shrimp*
> *1 cup bean sprouts, fresh or canned*
> *½ cup finely chopped onion*
> *½ cup thinly sliced celery*
> *3 tablespoons peanut oil, plus additional oil for frying*
> *6 eggs*
> *1 tablespoon cornstarch dissolved in 1 tablespoon imported soy sauce*
> *1 teaspoon salt*
> *Hot-pepper sauce*

Sauce

> *2 tablespoons cornstarch*
> *½ cup chicken broth*
> *2 teaspoons dry sherry*
> *1 tablespoon imported soy sauce*

Drain and flake the crab meat, or tip the shrimp into a sieve and rinse them under cold running water. If using canned bean sprouts, rinse them, too. Place the crab or shrimp and sprouts in a bowl. In a skillet sauté the onion and celery in peanut oil for 3 to 5 minutes, or until the vegetables are softened, and add them and about 1 tablespoon of oil from the skillet to the sprouts mixture, discarding the remaining oil. In another bowl beat the eggs until well mixed. Add the cornstarch mixture, salt, and hot-pepper sauce to the eggs. Mix well. Pour the egg mixture over the sprout mixture and combine thoroughly. Lightly coat a heavy skillet with oil. Place over medium-high heat and when hot, pour the batter ¼ cup at a time into the skillet. Cook the pancakes until they are browned. Turn and brown the other sides. Continue making pancakes a few at a time; do not crowd the pan. Keep the pancakes warm, covered on a platter, while you make the sauce.

In a saucepan mix together the cornstarch, chicken broth, sherry, and soy sauce, and bring the mixture to a boil, stirring. Cook the mixture over medium heat until the sauce thickens. Pour the sauce over the pancakes. Serves 4.

One-Eyed Texan

1 slice white bread, crusts removed
1 tablespoon butter or margarine
1 teaspoon vegetable oil
1 egg
Salt to taste
Worcestershire sauce to taste

With a 1½-inch cookie cutter cut a hole in the center of the bread slice. Heat the butter or margarine and oil in a small skillet until sizzling, and add the slice. Carefully break an egg into the hole. Fry the bread and egg for about 2 minutes, or until the underside of the bread is browned and the egg looks somewhat set, and flip both together with a spatula, being careful not to break the yolk. Fry the bread until that side, too, is browned, but the center of the egg is still runny—about 2 minutes. Sprinkle with salt and Worcestershire sauce to taste. Serves 1.

A small plate of quick-energy spaghetti for an active child.

CHAPTER SIX

Solid Satisfactions

Everyone gets the occasional craving for comfort food. Unfortunately, not many find much comfort in a carrot; it's likelier to be something dripping with butter or melted cheese. Dieters must resist the craving, but the rest of us can justify indulgence in a high-calorie snack by reasoning that a full meal could be even more fattening. Adults who are heavy eaters want bulk—not dainty snacks. Children crave—and their high level of activity often warrants—large doses of carbohydrates. For both, the recipes here have been chosen for sound nutrition (you'll find no empty calories!), hearty flavor, and spur-of-the-moment preparation.

Almost all cooked starches are delicious upon second appearance, not only leftover potatoes and cereals, which can be fried crisp, but rice and noodles, too. Fried Rice, tossed in a wok or skillet with remnants from Sunday's roast and oddments of cooked vegetables, actually requires leftover rice. Or take these three ingredients another way: rinse the vegetables if they are buttered, then marinate them, the meat scraps, and rice in a vinaigrette for an instant rice salad. Even an unpromising lump of cooked noodles yields to clever treatment. Sauté a handful of sliced mushrooms in butter and oil, add bread crumbs and let them brown, stir in a cup of rinsed cold noodles and heat them thoroughly. Or sauté slivered almonds, add additional butter, a tablespoon of poppy seeds, and a cup of rinsed noodles. Toss until heated, add a squeeze of lemon juice and some salt and pepper. Either way, you have a hot and unusual little dish in a very short time.

Waffled French Toast

If you use a waffle iron without a nonstick surface, lightly brush the grids with butter before baking.

For savory waffles that need no sweet topping, add 1 tablespoon of grated Parmesan or Romano cheese to the batter.

1 egg
¼ cup milk
1 tablespoon melted butter or margarine
⅛ teaspoon salt
2 to 3 slices bread

Heat the waffle iron. In a bowl just large enough to hold a bread slice, combine the egg, milk, butter or margarine, and salt, mixing with a fork or whisk until blended. Dip the slices, 1 at a time, in the batter until well coated. Bake the slices, testing after 2 minutes to see if the color is golden. Bake the toast longer if necessary. Serve with honey, syrup, or jam; or without a topping if cheese has been added to the batter. Serves 1 to 2.

English Muffin Pizzas

English muffins, halved and lightly toasted
Mozzarella cheese, sliced
Tomato slices
Oregano, pulverized
Salt and pepper to taste
Seven-Minute Tomato Sauce, p. 65, or canned
tomato sauce

On a baking sheet or tray lined with foil arrange the muffins. Top each half with a slice of cheese and tomato. Sprinkle with oregano, add salt and pepper to taste, and drizzle 2 teaspoons tomato sauce over each half. Broil the halves until the cheese is melted.

Greek Pizza

Top each muffin half with crumbled feta cheese and a dollop of ratatouille, p. 91. Broil until the cheese is melted.

Southwestern Pizza

Top each muffin half with 2 slices of Monterey Jack cheese, mild green Mexican pepper slices, drained, and 2 teaspoons of canned taco sauce. Broil until the cheese is melted.

Peanut Butter Pizza

Spread each muffin half thickly with peanut butter, top with crisp-cooked crumbled bacon, and broil until the peanut butter bubbles.

Croque Monsieur
(French Sautéed Sandwich)

"Croque" is French for "crackly." The sandwich is sautéed in oil and butter until the cheese is melted and the bread crisp.

2 slices firm bread, buttered
2 thin slices Swiss cheese
1 thin slice boiled or cooked ham
2 tablespoons butter or margarine
2 teaspoons vegetable oil

Layer a slice of bread, butter side up, with cheese, ham, and cheese. Lay the other slice of bread, butter side down, on top and press down firmly. Trim the crusts and press down again. In a skillet melt the butter or margarine and oil. Brown the sandwich slowly, about 3 minutes on each side. Makes 1 sandwich.

Croque Madame

The same as Monsieur, except that the ham is replaced by a thin slice of cooked chicken or turkey.

After School

At what age can children begin to function by themselves in the kitchen? A mother of six kids says that by the time they're old enough to go to school, they have the necessary dexterity and concentration to put together simple concoctions. However, she adds cynically, her criterion of who is old enough to cook stands in direct proportion to their ability to clean up. With that in mind, the snacks that children prepare best fall in certain categories—the ones with fewest ingredients and numbers of bowls or pans needed, or amount of mess to be expected.

Baby Baked Potatoes are simplicity itself; English Muffin Pizzas can be put together by children still too young to use the stove (an adult does the actual broiling). Another filling do-it-yourself after-school idea is to prepare noodles or pasta while the kids prepare side dishes of butter or margarine, chopped nuts, parsley, grated Parmesan or shredded cheddar cheese, shredded boiled ham or even cottage cheese, cinnamon and sugar. They can then sprinkle or spoon on these healthy flavorings over the cooked pasta according to their tastes.

Economy is a positive reason for helping children learn to make their own snacks. Labor costs are a large part of the price of any prepared, premixed, or packaged food. When the young ones cook from scratch, free child labor cuts costs considerably. As for a big problem with most kids—an unrestrained appetite for sweets—any hungry child can reach for the cookies and ice cream. But the child with cooking skills has the alternative of making snacks that contain less sugar, more protein, and more vitamins and minerals. Besides the foods in this chapter, you might like your children to try the following:

Yogurt Fruit Crunch
Frozen Fruit Juice Pops
Sautéed Apple Slices
Sautéed Banana
Whole-Wheat Brownies
Oatmeal, Coconut, and Raisin Cookies
Trail Mix
Almond Granola

As soon as children are competent to deal with a hot oven they can bake a potato all by themselves—with no mess at all.

Herbed Spaghetti with Garlic

1 clove garlic, mashed
1 tablespoon olive oil or vegetable oil
1 tablespoon butter or margarine
¼ cup combined finely chopped fresh herbs,
*   such as green-onion tops or chives, fresh dill,*
*   watercress, or parsley*
Salt and pepper to taste
2 ounces thin spaghetti, cooked and drained

In a small saucepan sauté the garlic over medium heat in the oil until it is golden, remove, and discard it. Over low heat melt the butter or margarine in the oil, add the herbs, and salt and pepper to taste. Pour the sauce over the spaghetti and serve at once. Serves 1.

Fettucini Alfredo

2 tablespoons butter or margarine
2 ounces fettucini egg noodles, cooked and
*   drained*
2 tablespoons grated Parmesan cheese
1 tablespoon heavy cream or half-and-half
Salt and pepper to taste
Additional grated Parmesan

In a skillet large enough to hold the noodles, melt the butter or margarine over medium heat. Do not let it brown. Add the noodles, toss them gently, and add the cheese and cream or half-and-half. Toss again and serve at once. Add salt and pepper and grated Parmesan to taste. Serves 1.

Linguine with White Clam Sauce

If there is an opened bottle of white vermouth in the house, use it for the wine called for in this recipe.

> *3 tablespoons olive oil or vegetable oil*
> *1 clove garlic, finely chopped*
> *¼ cup combined equal parts clam juice (drained*
>   *from the canned clams) and dry white wine*
> *1 6½-ounce can minced clams, drained*
> *Salt and pepper to taste*
> *1 tablespoon butter or margarine, softened*
> *4 ounces linguine or thin spaghetti, cooked and*
>   *drained*
> *1 tablespoon chopped parsley*

In a small saucepan heat the oil and sauté the garlic over medium heat for about 20 seconds or until it is golden. Do not let it burn. Pour in the clam-juice-and-wine mixture and boil until the liquid is reduced by half. Add the clams, stir until they are heated through, and add salt and pepper to taste. Swirl in the butter or margarine. Immediately toss the linguine with the sauce and sprinkle it with chopped parsley. Serve at once. Serves 2.

Sautéed Cereal

Sautéed-grain fans often make extra amounts of breakfast cereals in order to have some left over to enjoy this treat. Or, cook breakfast cereals solely for this purpose. In the north of Italy, sautéed cornmeal mush goes by the name of polenta, and is served with Tomato Sauce, p. 65, optional, and grated Parmesan cheese and butter.

> *1½ cups cooked cereal, such as farina, grits, or*
>   *yellow cornmeal, made according to instruc-*
>   *tions on label*

While still warm, spread the cereal in a buttered 8-inch pie plate. When cold, cut into wedges or squares and sauté in butter or margarine until browned, about 3 to 4 minutes on each side. Serve with butter and honey, or syrup.

Seven-Minute Tomato Sauce

There are three ways to be sure you have tomato sauce when you want it: keep cans of tomato sauce in the pantry, cook tomato sauce in quantity and store it in small containers in the freezer, or whip it up just as the craving strikes you. Unlike most tomato sauces, which simmer for hours to develop smooth texture and flavor, this quick version has bright color, fresh flavor, and a pleasantly rough texture.

1 tablespoon olive oil or vegetable oil
1 clove garlic, crushed
1 1-pound can imported Italian toma-
toes, drained and crushed
Pinch of sugar
Salt and pepper to taste
1 tablespoon chopped fresh basil or
chopped parsley, or more to taste

In a saucepan heat the oil and sauté the garlic over medium heat, stirring, until it is golden. Add the tomatoes. Simmer the sauce, uncovered, for 7 minutes, stirring occasionally. Add sugar, and salt and pepper to taste. Just before serving remove the garlic and stir in the chopped basil or parsley. Makes 1 cup.

Sweet and Sour Bean Salad

This salad will keep for several weeks in the refrigerator, covered with plastic wrap. Serve as is, or stuff it, partially drained, into pita pockets.

1 cup each of the following canned beans, drained in a sieve and rinsed under cold running water: green beans, wax beans, kidney beans, chick-peas (ceci or garbanzos)
1 cup chopped green pepper
½ cup chopped pimientos
½ cup chopped green onions, including some of the green tops
¼ cup chopped celery
Salt and pepper to taste

Dressing

1 cup cider vinegar
1 cup sugar
¼ cup water
2 teaspoons prepared horseradish

Make the dressing: in a saucepan combine the vinegar, sugar, water, and horseradish, bring the mixture to a boil, and simmer it for 5 minutes, or until the sugar is dissolved and the dressing is somewhat syrupy. In a large salad bowl combine the beans and other vegetables, pour the dressing over them, and mix the salad thoroughly. Add salt and pepper to taste. Chill the salad well before serving. Makes about 6 cups.

Bulgur Wheat

Bulgur, also called burghul, is a quickly prepared staple of Middle Eastern cooking, used much like rice. Softened in water, it swells to almost four times its dry size. It is sold at Middle Eastern markets and in health-food stores.

> *¼ cup bulgur wheat*
> *Boiling water*

In a heatproof bowl cover the bulgur with boiling water and let it soften for 10 minutes, stirring occasionally. Test for doneness; if the grains are still somewhat hard, add a little boiling water, and let them swell for 5 minutes longer. Tip the bulgur into a sieve and drain it. Serve hot with butter and a sprinkling of salt, with leftover cold meat, or topped with Ratatouille, p. 91. Serves 1.

Tabbouleh

> *1 cup softened bulgur wheat (see above), cooled*
> *1 cup chopped fresh vegetables, such as ripe tomato, cucumber, onion, parsley*
> *½ teaspoon salt*
> *2 tablespoons lemon juice*
> *2 tablespoons olive oil, or to taste*
> *1 tablespoon chopped fresh mint or ½ teaspoon crumbled dried mint*

In a bowl combine all ingredients and toss gently. Serves 1 to 2.

Stir-Fried Meat and Vegetables

1½ tablespoons vegetable oil, preferably peanut
½ clove garlic, minced
1 slice fresh gingerroot, peeled and minced (or substitute a pinch of dried ground ginger)
1 cup cooked chicken, pork, ham, or beef, cut into ½-inch cubes
1 cup cooked vegetables, cut into ¼- to ½-inch slices or cubes
1 tablespoon thinly sliced green onion, including some of the green top (optional)

Sauce

½ teaspoon cornstarch
1 teaspoon sherry
1 teaspoon soy sauce, preferably imported
¼ cup chicken broth

Make the sauce. In a small measuring pitcher, combine the cornstarch with the sherry and the dried ground ginger if you are using it, and stir to a smooth paste. Add the soy sauce and chicken broth and set aside.

Heat the wok or skillet over high heat until a drop of water sizzles on its surface. Pour in the oil and continue heating until the oil is hot but not smoking. Add the garlic and fresh ginger, and stir until golden. Pour in the meat and vegetables all at once, and stir fry for 1 minute, or until they are just heated through. Restir the cornstarch mixture, and pour it around the rim of the pan. Continue to stir fry until the sauce thickens. Remove from flame, garnish with green onion and serve at once. Serves 2.

Stir-Frying

The technique called stir-frying was invented thousands of years ago in China as a means to cook food rapidly while using the least amount of fuel possible—not a bad idea in these days, either. Meat and vegetables are cut into uniform small bits and tossed rapidly in a wok or skillet; each facet of the food makes momentary contact with the heated oil and is instantly sealed. The morsels are moved so rapidly that they are never permitted to stick, or to steam. Stir-frying is an excellent way to deal with leftovers—they cook only long enough to heat through.

Most essential flavorings and ingredients can be found on supermarket shelves, such as peanut oil (preferred by most stir-fry cooks), cornstarch, water chestnuts, bamboo shoots, and bean sprouts. Do make an effort to find imported soy sauce: it is infinitely superior to domestic products. Leftover vegetables may be broccoli, cauliflower, green or red pepper, asparagus, string beans, peas, carrots, cabbage, or spinach. Vegetables are best if they have been cooked crisp, rather than soft. Rinse the vegetables and drain on paper towels. Canned bamboo shoots or sliced water chestnuts, and fresh or canned bean sprouts can be added right along with the leftover vegetables. Pork and chicken are the preferred meats, but leftover ham or beef are good too.

A one-handled wok is the easiest kind for a novice stir-fryer to handle. The stir frying instrument is called a wok chan, but if you use a skillet, a spatula works well. Wok or skillet should be heated over high heat until a drop of water sizzles on its surface before adding oil.

When the oil is very hot but not smoking, add the minced garlic and ginger and stir for 1 minute, or until golden. Then add the meat and vegetables. Stir fry vigorously by lifting the ingredients from the bottom and dropping them back, turning the pan as you lift and toss so no food stays in contact with the pan for more than a couple of seconds at a time. Stir fry only until the ingredients are heated through.

Restir the sauce and pour it in a circular motion inside the rim of the pan. Continue to stir fry the meat and vegetables in the sauce over medium heat until the liquid clears and thickens.

Fried Rice

The secret to successful fried rice is the age of the cooked rice used; it must be at least a day old, so that it has dried out enough to fry. One cup of cooked rice may not seem enough for an ample snack for two, but with the addition of other ingredients, it really is.

> *3 tablespoons vegetable oil, preferably peanut*
> *1 egg, lightly beaten*
> *1 tablespoon chopped red or green pepper*
> *1 tablespoon chopped green onion, including some of the green top*
> *¼ cup shredded cabbage or cooked chopped vegetables*
> *¼ cup drained canned shrimp, or cooked shredded meat, such as ham, chicken, or pork*
> *1 cup cold cooked rice*
> *Imported soy sauce to taste*

In a wok or skillet heat 1 tablespoon oil. When it sizzles, quickly scramble the egg, remove it, and set aside on a plate. Add the remaining oil, pepper, and green onion and stir-fry for 1 minute. Add the cabbage and shrimp or meat and stir-fry until the cabbage wilts slightly; it should still be crisp when served. (If using cooked vegetables, add them after adding the cooked meat.) Add the rice and stir-fry until it is heated through. Add 1 tablespoon soy sauce and return the egg to the pan, breaking it up and mixing it well. Serve at once with more soy sauce to taste. Serves 2.

Baby Baked Potatoes

> *Small baking potatoes, about 2½ inches long*
> *Salt to taste*

Preheat the oven to 500 degrees. Pierce the potatoes all over with a fork. (At this heat, unpierced potatoes can build up enough steam to explode.) Bake the potatoes for 30 minutes, or until the skin is crisp and the center is tender when tested with a knife or skewer. Serve with salt, and if you wish add butter, sour cream, or chives.

Macaroni Salad

Use any type of pasta for the salad, such as shells, ziti, riga-toni, bowties, or elbow macaroni. Exact proportions for vege-tables and other additions—chopped stuffed olives, drained and flaked tuna fish, or strips of leftover meat—need not be precise as long as the salad is well bound with mayonnaise.

> *1 cup cooked pasta*
> *1 teaspoon cider vinegar or lemon juice*
> *1 teaspoon spicy brown, Dijon-type, lemon, or green peppercorn mustard*
> *1 tablespoon mayonnaise, or to taste*
> *1 tablespoon finely chopped or grated onion, chives, or green onions, including some of the green top*
> *¼ cup combined chopped raw vegetables, such as celery, parsley, or tomato, or leftover cooked vegetables, such as green beans, zuc-chini, or broccoli*
> *1 tablespoon chopped pimiento*
> *Salt and pepper to taste*

In a salad bowl combine all the ingredients and mix well. Serves 2.

Picnic Potato Salad

Keep this salad (and most any others) cold on an excursion. It is also delicious served hot.

> *1 pound small red or yellow new potatoes*
> *4 tablespoons Vinaigrette, p. 84*
> *1 teaspoon spicy brown mustard*
> *½ teaspoon salt*
> *1 tablespoon chopped onion or green onion, in-cluding some of the green top*
> *1 tablespoon chopped dill pickle*
> *3 slices crisp cooked bacon, crumbled*
> *1 tablespoon chopped parsley*

In a saucepan boil the potatoes in their jackets until they are tender when pierced with a knife. Make the dressing: in a bowl combine the Vinaigrette, mustard, and salt and mix well. Add the green onion, pickle, and bacon. When the potatoes are cooked, peel them under cool running water and slice them into a bowl. Pour the dressing over the warm slices of potatoes, mix gently to coat each slice, and sprinkle with chopped parsley. Serve the salad at once or refrigerate it. Let chilled salad return to room temperature before serving. Serves 2.

Friendly Starches

Starchy foods have been sadly misunderstood. They are not necessarily "empty" calories, and are often not even particularly high in calories. A 5-ounce potato contains about 110 calories; a 5-ounce steak contains 500 calories. Empty calories are those in foods that supply no nutrients. That same potato supplies 20 percent of the daily vitamin C needed in our diet, as well as other essential nutrients.

To be sure you are getting the most out of the carbohydrates you use, look for the word *enriched* on the label, and read what nutrients have been added. Many stores carry pasta and macaroni products that are enriched or to which such healthy ingredients as wheat germ have been added. There are also whole-wheat pastas and spinach noodles that may be a healthy choice. Brown rice, because the outer coating with all its vitamins has not been removed, is a good source of fiber as well as being nutritious. Crushed whole wheat, or bulgur, is full of good things—including some fiber needed for good intestinal functioning. Beans, dried and precooked or canned, are one of the few vegetable foods that provide large quantities of the proteins found in meat and fish. Much as we need protein, it is estimated that we consume double the quantity we can use.

Rice Salad

> *1 cup cold cooked rice*
> *3 finely chopped green onions, including some*
> *of the green tops*
> *Thin strips of raw carrot or green pepper*
> *Thin strips of cooked poultry, beef, pork, or ham*
> *(optional)*
> *5 pimiento-stuffed green olives, chopped*
> *2 tablespoons Vinaigrette, p. 84, or to taste*
> *Salt and pepper to taste*

In a serving bowl combine all the ingredients and toss them gently. If you like, add a small amount of dried or fresh herbs, such as thyme, marjoram, or tarragon. Serve at once or chill, covered. Serves 2.

Crepes

If 2 crepes are all you want, keep the remaining batter covered with plastic wrap in the refrigerator until the following day. Stir the batter well before using and if it seems thick, thin it with a teaspoon of water. The easiest way to make crepes is in an 8-inch nonstick skillet.

> *1 egg*
> *$\frac{1}{3}$ cup milk*
> *$\frac{1}{3}$ cup flour*
> *$\frac{1}{8}$ teaspoon salt*
> *1 tablespoon butter or margarine, melted*
> *1 tablespoon water*

In a bowl blend the egg lightly with a fork, add the milk, flour, and salt, and beat the mixture for a few moments more until it is fairly smooth. (It is all right if some very small lumps remain.) Add the butter or margarine, beat to incorporate, and thin the batter with water.

Heat the skillet over fairly high heat until a drop of water sizzles when flicked on the surface. (If you are not using a nonstick skillet, swirl a bit of butter in the pan before making each crepe.) Stir the batter. Pour a scant $\frac{1}{4}$ cup into the skillet and swirl the skillet until the bottom is covered. Cook until the surface of the crepe is fairly dry and small bubbles

To prevent fillings from oozing out the ends of a rolled crepe, fold the sides of each crepe in first, then roll it up into a neat package.

appear. Slip a spatula under the crepe. If it lifts easily, flip it, and cook the other side for about 30 seconds. Slide the crepe onto a plate. Serves 1 or 2.

Crepes with Ham and Cheese

Preheat the oven to 350 degrees. Roll the crepes around thin slices of boiled ham and Swiss cheese and place, seam side down, in a small baking pan. Heat the crepes on the middle rack of the oven for 5 minutes, or until the cheese is melted.

Crepes with Asparagus and Dill

Preheat the oven to 350 degrees. Roll each crepe around 1 or 2 drained canned asparagus spears and sprinkle the asparagus with chopped fresh dill or dried dill pulverized between the palms of the hand. (Use ½ teaspoon of fresh dill or a generous pinch of dried dill for each crepe.) Place the crepes, seam side down, in a small baking pan and heat them on the middle rack of the oven for 5 minutes.

Crepes with Red Caviar and Sour Cream

Spread 1 tablespoon each of red caviar and sour cream down the center of each freshly made crepe and roll it up. Eat at once, while the crepes are still warm.

A muffin snack, made quickly using Homemade Biscuit Mix.

CHAPTER SEVEN

Quick Breads

Prepared cake, cookie, and coffee-cake mixes (some are so complete they even come with a disposable pan) are fine products for special uses. Though expensive, they certainly simplify snack preparation at the country place, the ski shack, or aboard the boat—any site where stocking bakery basics is inconvenient. They are best when eaten shortly after they emerge from the oven.

There are helpful aids to quick baked goods, though, that lie between the extremes of "just add water and love" and recipes so purist that you are all but instructed to grow your own wheat, and then grind it. Frozen pie dough keeps well and defrosts quickly. Little children get a kick out of cutting it into fancy shapes, sprinkling them with sugar and cinnamon, and proudly watching their own creations emerge from the oven. Use piecrust mix for the same purpose. Gingerbread mix is improved by substituting orange or apple juice for the water called for in the instructions. Besides mixes, you may want to keep a couple of special breads in the freezer for impromptu snacking. A few ideas are whole-wheat bread, buttered and spread with applesauce, sprinkled with brown sugar; cocktail rye, spread with cream cheese and chutney; Boston brown bread (available in cans), with peanut butter and chopped dates; rye, pumpernickel, or whole-grain breads topped with cheddar or Muenster cheese and melted under the broiler. Some love that last one with drained sauerkraut on top.

Stale French or Italian bread, or even hard rolls or hero loaves, make perfectly good garlic bread. A way to use plain white sandwich bread when it has become stale is to fry it. Trim off the crusts and cut the bread in strips. Melt butter in a skillet, and fry the strips over medium heat, turning once, until both sides are crisp and golden.

The word *quick*, when used in quick bread, is a comparative term. Although there is no waiting for dough to rise in these nonyeast recipes, the loaf breads take 35 minutes to an hour to bake. They are tasty snacks, but you may want to plan ahead for them.

Garlic Bread

To use a stale French or Italian bread for this recipe, slice it thickly, brown one side of the slices under the broiler, then spread the garlic butter on the other side, sprinkle with Parmesan and paprika, and brown the second side.

> *1 small clove garlic*
> *4 tablespoons butter or margarine, softened*
> *1 8-inch loaf Italian or French bread, or 2 hard rolls*
> *Grated Parmesan cheese*
> *Paprika*

Preheat the oven to 450 degrees. In a small bowl press the garlic through a garlic press into the butter or margarine and mix well to blend. Make diagonal cuts in the bread or rolls 1 inch apart, but do not cut all the way through the loaf or rolls. Spread the butter or margarine generously between the slices and on top of the bread. Sprinkle with cheese and paprika and bake for 10 minutes. Serves 2.

Caraway Scones

> *2 cups biscuit mix*
> *1 teaspoon caraway seeds*
> *4 tablespoons butter or margarine*
> *⅔ cup buttermilk*

Preheat the oven to 450 degrees. In a small mixing bowl combine the biscuit mix, caraway seeds, and the butter or margarine and, using your fingertips, mix until the mixture forms particles the size of peas. Add the buttermilk and stir only enough to moisten the batter. Spoon the batter evenly onto an ungreased baking sheet to form 2 cakes 5 inches in diameter. Make a crisscross indentation on each cake with a knife dipped in flour. Bake the cakes for 10 to 12 minutes, or until they are well browned and light. Remove to a rack and break each cake into 4 scones. Split and serve hot with butter. Leftover scones can be wrapped in plastic wrap and frozen. Serve them split, toasted, and spread with marmalade or honey. Makes 8.

Banana Bread

This is a very moist, spongy bread that stays fresh several days if wrapped airtight in plastic wrap.

> *1¼ cups flour*
> *1 cup sugar*
> *½ teaspoon salt*
> *1 teaspoon baking soda*
> *½ cup solid vegetable shortening*
> *2 fully ripe medium bananas*
> *2 eggs*

Preheat the oven to 350 degrees. Sift the flour, sugar, salt, and baking soda into a bowl. In a blender blend the vegetable shortening, bananas, and eggs and add the mixture to the dry ingredients. Mix only enough to moisten the dry ingredients. Spoon the batter into a lightly buttered and floured 9-inch-square baking pan and bake for 35 to 40 minutes, or until a toothpick inserted in the center comes out clean. Remove the bread from the oven and let it stand in the pan for 5 minutes. Loosen the edges with a spatula and turn the bread out on a rack covered with waxed paper. Let the bread cool to room temperature before cutting into squares. To make without a blender: Add the shortening to the sifted dry ingredients and cut it as for piecrust. Mash the bananas, beat the eggs well, and add to the dry ingredients. Proceed as directed above. Makes 1 loaf.

Homemade Biscuit Mix

Those who have the personality—and the space—to prepare and store premixed bases for snacks might like to try this basic biscuit mix. It tastes better than commercial products and it can be used both for biscuits and muffins. Because it contains shortening as well as dry ingredients, it must be frozen or refrigerated, but using the mix should cut your preparation time down to as little as 5 minutes.

12 cups sifted flour
2 tablespoons salt
4 tablespoons baking powder
2 cups shortening: butter, margarine, solid vegetable shortening, lard, or a combination, at room temperature

In a large bowl sift together the dry ingredients, sifting ¼ of each quantity at a time. With a pastry blender or 2 knives, cut the shortening into the dry ingredients until the mixture has the consistency of cornmeal. Divide the dough and pack it into freezer containers. The dough will keep in the freezer for 6 months or for 1 month in the refrigerator.

To use for 6 Biscuits
1 cup biscuit mix at room temperature
¼ to ⅓ cup milk

Preheat the oven to 450 degrees. In a bowl combine the milk with the dough, tossing with a fork until it is soft but not sticky. On a floured surface roll the dough out ¾ inch thick and cut out biscuits with a cookie cutter. Place them on an ungreased baking sheet and bake on the middle rack of the oven for 12 to 15 minutes.

Cheese Biscuits: Add ½ cup shredded cheddar cheese to the dough.

Orange Biscuits: Before baking, dent the top of each biscuit with a spoon and add a dab of orange marmalade.

To use for 6 Muffins
1 cup biscuit mix at room temperature
1 tablespoon sugar
1 egg, well beaten
½ cup milk

Preheat the oven to 400 degrees. In a bowl, combine all the ingredients, but stir only enough to dampen the dough. Grease muffin tin, and fill cups ⅔ full. Bake on the middle rack of the oven for 15 minutes.

Blueberry Muffins: Add ½ cup blueberries lightly coated with flour to the batter before baking.

Date Muffins: Add ¼ cup pitted dates, sliced and lightly coated with flour, to the batter before baking.

Orange Muffins: Add ½ cup diced candied orange peel, lightly coated with flour, to the batter before baking.

Nut Muffins: Add ¼ cup chopped pecans or walnuts to the batter before baking.

Date-Bran Bread

1 cup all-purpose flour
1 cup whole-wheat flour
1½ cups whole bran cereal
1 teaspoon salt
2 teaspoons baking powder
½ teaspoon baking soda
½ cup dark molasses
1½ cups milk
1 egg, well beaten
4 tablespoons butter or margarine, melted
1 cup finely chopped pitted dates

Preheat the oven to 350 degrees. In a large bowl mix the first 6 ingredients. Stir in the remaining ingredients. Mix only enough to moisten the dry ingredients. Pour the batter into a buttered 9-by-5-by-3-inch loaf pan and bake for 1 hour. Turn the loaf out on a rack and let it cool before slicing. Makes 1 loaf.

Applesauce Brown Bread

2 cups whole-wheat flour
1 cup cornmeal
¾ teaspoon salt
1 teaspoon baking soda
1 cup buttermilk
1 cup dark molasses
¾ cup applesauce
¾ cup raisins

Preheat the oven to 350 degrees. In a large bowl combine the first 4 ingredients. Add the buttermilk and molasses and beat with a spoon until the mixture is smooth. Fold in the applesauce and raisins and spread the batter in a buttered 9-inch square baking pan and bake it 35 minutes or until a toothpick inserted in the center comes out clean. Cut the bread into squares and serve hot with butter. Makes 1 loaf.

In a few minutes, fresh vegetables can be transformed into a snack of Crudités.

CHAPTER EIGHT
Salads & Vegetables

There is no substitute for fruits and vegetables freshly picked at the height of their color, flavor, and texture. Don't be embarrassed to poke cucumbers and eggplants to check for firmness, snap a green bean to test for freshness, taste peas to see if they are sweet, or sniff a melon to see if it is ripe. If such produce seems promising, by all means buy it. Keep canned or frozen products in the pantry or freezer to tide you over days when you have no time to shop, or top-quality produce is not available.

With a little help, canned vegetables make quick, nutritious refections that can be very good indeed. Buy the smallest sizes available, to be used in one go, with no leftovers to worry about. Drain them in a sieve and rinse them under cold water for fresher flavor. Most such vegetables taste best when served at room temperature. Try green beans as the French eat them, with lots and lots of chopped garlic and perhaps a little oil and vinegar. Dip artichoke hearts or asparagus spears into Blue Cheese Dressing. Pickled beets are great as is, with perhaps a squeeze of lemon juice, and so is the eggplant "caviar" called caponata. Canned kidney beans, black-eyed peas, chick-peas, and limas are excellent for salads. Canned fruits are useful in salads, too, and make good snacks all by themselves.

Frozen vegetables don't come in the tiny quantities canned vegetables do, but they do offer fresher flavor, texture, and color. To use only part of a package, take it from the freezer and bang it hard on the table or counter. This will usually break the frozen vegetables apart so you can remove what you need from the package. Don't just put the remainder back in the freezer, however. To prevent drying, the remain-

Salad Dressings

With this vocabulary of six salad dressings, you can dress everything from leftover string beans to fresh-off-the-tree fruits. In fact, they are used as well for Rice Salad (p. 73), Poultry Salad (p. 28), and other fine snacks mentioned elsewhere. With the exception of those that contain fresh ingredients such as chives or onion, these dressings—doubled or even tripled to save time—can be stored for weeks tightly covered in the refrigerator. Keep Blue Cheese and Russian dressings no more than a few days, as even under refrigeration, fresh ingredients become soggy and off-flavored.

Vinaigrette (French Dressing)

2 tablespoons wine vinegar or cider vinegar, or lemon juice
1 teaspoon Dijon-type mustard or spicy brown mustard
½ teaspoon salt
6 tablespoons olive oil or vegetable oil
Pepper to taste

In a bowl combine the vinegar or lemon juice, mustard, and salt, and whisk to blend. Add the oil and pepper to taste and whisk vigorously. Use with any fresh greens, to marinate rinsed, leftover vegetables, or as a dressing for canned vegetables. Makes ½ cup.

Blue Cheese Dressing

½ cup Vinaigrette
1 tablespoon crumbled blue cheese or Roquefort cheese, or to taste
1 teaspoon finely chopped shallot, chives, onion, or green onion

In a bowl combine all the ingredients. Use with any fresh greens, over rinsed leftover vegetables, or as a dressing for canned vegetables. Makes about ½ cup.

Russian Dressing

½ cup mayonnaise
2 tablespoons chili sauce or catsup
1 teaspoon prepared horseradish
Worcestershire sauce to taste
½ to 1 teaspoon finely chopped or grated onion

In a bowl combine all the ingredients and mix thoroughly. Use with crunchy greens such as iceberg lettuce, as a dressing for shellfish, and as a spread for meat sandwiches. Makes ½ cup.

Chinese Dressing

1 tablespoon rice vinegar or white wine vinegar
1 teaspoon sugar
½ teaspoon ground ginger
1 tablespoon soy sauce
2 tablespoons vegetable oil, preferably peanut

In a bowl combine the vinegar, sugar, ginger, and soy sauce, and whisk to dissolve the sugar. Stir in the oil. Use as a dressing for light salads, such as bean sprouts or cucumbers. Makes about ¼ cup.

Yogurt-Mint Dressing

1 cup plain yogurt
2 tablespoons honey
1 teaspoon lemon juice
1 teaspoon dried mint, pulverized

In a bowl combine all the ingredients and blend vigorously. This dressing goes wonderfully with any combination of fresh fruit. Makes about 1¼ cup.

ing vegetables should be put in a plastic bag, sealed by twisting the top and securing it with a tie before being replaced in the freezer.

Although fresh vegetables are important for many recipes, you will also find here refreshing ways to use leftover vegetables in both cold and hot dishes.

Cucumber Raita
(Indian Cucumber and Yogurt Relish)

½ teaspoon mustard seeds
2 teaspoons vegetable oil
1 small cucumber, peeled, seeded, and diced
1½ cups plain yogurt
2 teaspoons lemon or lime juice
½ teaspoon salt
1 teaspoon chopped fresh coriander (Chinese parsley) or chopped parsley
2 tablespoons crushed roasted peanuts

In a small skillet combine the mustard seeds and vegetable oil and heat the mixture, covered, over medium heat until the seeds pop. In a bowl mix the remaining ingredients (except the peanuts) with the seeds and oil and toss gently. Serve the salad chilled or at room temperature sprinkled with crushed peanuts. Serves 2.

Bean Sprout Salad

Lots of munching, few calories. Bean sprouts—mung or soy— or grain sprouts such as alfalfa—are rich in protein and vitamin C.

1 cup bean sprouts, fresh or canned, or fresh alfalfa sprouts
1 cup shredded salad greens
2 tablespoons chopped canned water chestnuts or peeled, seeded, and diced cucumber
2 tablespoons slivered green pepper
2 tablespoons dry-roasted peanuts
¼ cup Chinese Dressing, p. 84

If using canned bean sprouts, tip them into a sieve, rinse them under cold running water, and dry them on paper towels. In a large serving bowl combine all the ingredients and toss them with the dressing. Serves 1 to 2.

Mini Chef's Salad

Ham, chicken, turkey, and tongue are the traditional meats for chef's salad. If you have any or all on hand, fine, but you can substitute strips of bologna, mortadella, mild salami, or canned luncheon meat. You may also add sliced radishes, avocado, sliced fresh mushrooms, chopped celery, or croutons.

> *1 cup torn salad greens*
> *Strips of meat or poultry*
> *Strips of Swiss or cheddar cheese*
> *¼ cup Vinaigrette, p. 84*
> *1 tomato, quartered, or a few cherry tomatoes*
> *1 hard-cooked egg, quartered*

In a shallow bowl or on a small platter arrange the meat and cheese strips on the greens and sprinkle with Vinaigrette. Garnish the salad with the tomato and hard-boiled egg quarters. Serves 1.

Onion, Orange, and Olive Salad

This salad can also be deliciously dressed by adding ½ teaspoon curry powder to ½ cup mayonnaise.

> *1 cup watercress, washed and stemmed*
> *1 small red onion, thinly sliced*
> *2 navel oranges, peeled, trimmed of all white*
>   *membranes, and sliced*
> *¼ cup sliced pitted black olives*
> *¼ cup Vinaigrette, p. 84*

In a salad bowl lined with the watercress arrange the onion and orange slices. Garnish the salad with sliced black olives and serve it with the Vinaigrette on the side. Serves 2 to 3.

Slim Snacking

Who needs snacks the most? Ironically, the dieter. Taking frequent infusions of low-calorie foods—in small amounts—makes good sense both nutritionally and psychologically. It's important that the shrinking body be supplied with the vitamins, minerals, proteins, and other nutrients necessary to maintain health. And as for mental health, the dieter who feels deprived during the endless hours between scanty meals is apt to lose heart, be led into temptation, and binge. Five or six snacks per day—but no full meals—may mean the difference between a successful reducing plan and one that's a flop.

Many people think that because a food is "low-calorie" they can eat as much of it as they want. Sorry, but calories do add up. Take cottage cheese, for example. A glance at the nutritional information on a carton of low-fat cottage cheese informs us that a serving contains only 90 calories. That's the good news. The bad news comes with further reading: the recommended serving is only ½ cup, not the entire carton.

At the expensive reducing resorts known as "spas," the people in charge of food use illusion to make less seem like more. A sliced orange is artfully fanned out to cover the entire surface of a small plate, and you are encouraged to eat it in small bites, using a knife and fork. A few ounces of fruit drink are served in a huge crystal goblet, to be sipped with a spoon, not gulped. The reasoning is that attractive presentation and leisurely ingestion fool the eye and satisfy the appetite. These are tricks that anyone can apply at home.

You will have to use good sense in adapting even the salads in this section to dieting needs. Orange, Coconut, and Rosewater Salad is a diet winner—provided you use unsweetened coconut and no sugar! Yogurt-Mint Salad Dressing can be adjusted by cutting the honey in half or less; use the dressing on any fruit combination. Stuffed Mushrooms, on the other hand, are fine as is. Other recipes from other chapters that would suit a serious dieter, and still provide good nutrition, include:

Chewy Pork Cubes
Beef Jerky
Crudités
Tzatziki
Consommé Bellevue
Harlequin Broth
Turkish Treat
Steak Tartare
Pita Stuffers (without the pita!)
Beef or Pork Teriyaki Srips
Cottage Cheese Variations
Omelets
Frittatas
Banana Slim Shake
Turkish Ayran
Ginger Buttermilk

A large goblet stretches out the pleasure of a low-calorie snack like Banana Slim Shake.

Orange, Coconut, and Rosewater Salad

Rosewater is a flowery flavoring found in Indian and Middle Eastern grocery shops as well as in some pharmacies. If unavailable, substitute dry sherry.

> 2 navel oranges, peeled, trimmed of all white membranes, and sliced
> 1 tablespoon confectioners' sugar
> 2 tablespoons packaged shredded coconut, preferably unsweetened
> Rosewater or dry sherry to taste

On a plate or in a shallow bowl arrange the orange slices, overlapping them slightly. Sprinkle them with sugar, coconut, and rosewater or dry sherry to taste. Chill the salad before serving. (If in a hurry, place the salad in the freezer for 5 minutes.) Serves 1 to 2.

Apple-Grape Salad

> 2 large unpeeled eating apples, cored and cut into bite-size pieces
> Juice of ½ lemon
> 1 small bunch seedless grapes or red grapes, halved and seeded
> ¼ to ½ cup coarsely chopped walnuts or blanched almonds
> ½ cup Yogurt-Mint Salad Dressing, p. 84

In a serving bowl sprinkle the apple pieces with lemon juice. (It keeps them from darkening.) Add the grapes, chopped nuts, and dressing, mixing well. Chill the salad before serving. (If in a hurry, place the salad in the freezer for 5 minutes.) Serves 2.

Stuffed Mushrooms

The filling here can also be used with small canned artichoke hearts.

> *1 12-ounce package fresh mushrooms, or 2 6-ounce cans mushroom crowns*
> *8 ounces cottage cheese*
> *2 tablespoons minced chives*
> *Dash of hot-pepper sauce*
> *¼ teaspoon Worcestershire sauce*
> *½ teaspoon celery salt*
> *½ teaspoon dry mustard*

If using fresh mushrooms, wipe them with a damp towel and remove the stems. With canned mushrooms, drain them and hollow them slightly with a grapefruit spoon. In a bowl combine the remaining ingredients and fill each mushroom crown with some of the mixture. Makes about 24.

Sautéed Cherry Tomatoes

Cherry tomatoes heat through very quickly. To keep them from bursting, grasp the handle of the skillet, and tilt it so that the tomatoes roll. Keep them in constant motion. The pinch of sugar below counteracts the natural acidity of the tomatoes and adds an attractive glaze.

> *1 tablespoon olive oil*
> *½ cup cherry tomatoes, washed and stemmed*
> *Pinch of sugar*
> *Salt and pepper to taste*
> *¼ teaspoon finely chopped garlic*
> *Chopped fresh basil or parsley*

In a small skillet heat the olive oil over medium heat. Add the tomatoes and roll them, tilting the skillet, until they begin to soften. Sprinkle them with sugar and continue rolling them until they show a slight glaze, at which point they will be cooked through. Add salt and pepper to taste and the garlic. Do not let the garlic brown, as it and the oil are served with the tomatoes. Garnish the tomatoes with basil or parsley and serve. Serves 1.

Stuff a Tomato

Winter tomatoes are really not worth bothering with, but during the summer when tomatoes are red, juicy, tasty, and plentiful, they can be prepared with a variety of stuffings for an attractive and wholesome snack.

To prepare the tomato, cut off about the top ¾ inch. With a spoon, scoop out the seeds and soft pulp inside so that you are left with the fleshy shell. Stuff the scooped-out tomato with one of the tuna fish variations on pp. 42–43; Ratatouille, p. 91, seasoned with bits of crumbled cooked bacon; or Sweet and Sour Bean Salad on p. 65. You could also adapt any of the stuffed egg recipes on p. 53 by chopping the whites coarsely, and stirring them into the yolk mixture. For a snack that could be mistaken for a meal, stuff tomatoes with curried or creamed leftover meats, pp. 35 and 36, and bake in the oven at 350 degrees for 20 minutes. Dieters can fall back on tomatoes stuffed with summery cottage cheese mixtures, p. 48.

Ratatouille
(French Vegetable Stew)

This hearty dish from the south of France is delicious hot or at room temperature. It freezes well for up to 6 weeks; freeze small portions and reheat them to serve with English Muffin Pizzas, p. 60, or polenta on p. 64. In season you may substitute peeled chopped fresh ripe tomatoes for canned. Measurements are given as a guide, but you need not be so precise. Use less or more of any vegetable, as you prefer. The object is to arrive at a nice balance of vegetable flavors.

> *2 tablespoons olive oil*
> *2 cups combined chopped fresh vegetables, preferably seeded green pepper, onion, zucchini, and eggplant*
> *1 clove garlic, chopped*
> *1 cup canned tomatoes, preferably imported Italian*
> *1 teaspoon salt*
> *½ teaspoon sugar*
> *1 small bay leaf*
> *½ teaspoon dried thyme*
> *¼ cup chopped parsley*

In a heavy pan heat the olive oil, add the green pepper and onion (if they are being used), and cook for 5 minutes, stirring occasionally, until the onion is translucent. Add the zucchini, eggplant, garlic, and tomatoes, breaking up the tomatoes with a wooden spoon. Stir in the salt, sugar, bay leaf, and thyme. Bring the ratatouille to a boil, uncovered. Lower the heat and simmer it for 20 minutes, or until vegetables are cooked through but somewhat crisp, stirring occasionally to prevent sticking. Remove the bay leaf and stir in the parsley. Makes about 2 cups.

Hollandaise Sauce

Hollandaise, troublesome to make for a dinner party of 20, is simplicity itself as a sauce for 1 or 2. Fanciful rumors to the contrary, it takes more effort to curdle hollandaise than to complete it successfully—in about 5 minutes! Once assured that this elegant sauce presents no real hazards, you can use it to artfully improve not only left-over asparagus, broccoli, or cauliflower, but to create that famous egg dish called Eggs Benedict. In this rich snack, poached eggs, topped with hollandaise, are served over a thin slice of strong-tasting ham (such as Westphalian) on a toasted English muffin. Vegetables are also good that way, or the ham can be left out and toast substituted for the muffin.

Use a double boiler for the sauce, making sure the water in the bottom portion does not touch the top portion. A whisk is the best utensil for beating the sauce as it cooks.

½ cup butter, preferably sweet, chilled
2 egg yolks
1 tablespoon lemon juice or tarragon vinegar

Put a small amount of water into the bottom portion of a double boiler and bring it to a boil over medium heat. Cut the butter in chunks into the top of the double boiler, and add the egg yolks and lemon juice. Turn the heat to as low as possible, and place the top portion of the double boiler over the bottom portion. With a whisk, stir the sauce constantly as it heats. The water should not be boiling; if you can't keep the heat low enough, turn it off altogether. Continue stirring until the sauce thickens into a smooth, thick cream. Remove the top of the double boiler and serve. The sauce can also be set aside and served lukewarm, if you need time to finish other preparations.

Butter, egg yolks, and lemon juice can be put into the top of the double boiler straight from the refrigerator.

After the small amount of water in the bottom of the double boiler has come to a boil, lower the heat to the lowest possible setting. Put the top of the double boiler in place and stir the ingredients constantly with a whisk. As the butter softens, whisk vigorously, being sure to scrape thickening sauce from the sides of the double boiler. Turning the heat off altogether as the sauce begins to thicken will avoid the possibility of curdling.

The Hollandaise is done when it is nearly as thick as sour cream. If the rest of the snack isn't ready yet, keep the sauce warm over hot tap water in the double boiler.

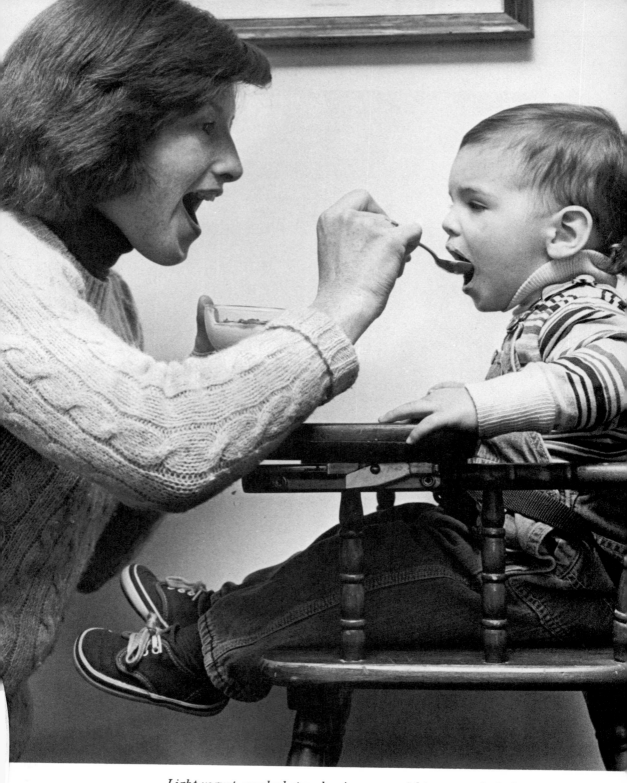

Light yogurt, crushed strawberries—a nourishing sweet for babies, a slimming one for parents.

CHAPTER NINE
Sweets

A well-stocked sweets cabinet equips you to go to work when the sweet tooth gnaws, day or night. With ginger, chocolate, or lemon wafers on hand, you have the base for ice-box cake.

This concoction is made by smearing homemade or prepared whipped cream over each wafer in turn, stacking them 6 to 8 wafers high, and placing the layered "cake" in the refrigerator. Within a few hours, the wafers absorb enough moisture from the cream so the cake can be cut into slices, or eaten whole with a fork. S'mores, an old childhood favorite, can't be made without graham crackers. Cereal Chocolate Clusters, a homemade substitute for allowance-depleting candy bars, require puffed wheat, rice, or oat cereal.

If sundaes are your weakness, have on hand a few jars of ice-cream toppings and nuts in syrup. You'll want apricot jelly for Hungarian pancakes, or try currant jelly. Other things never to run out of: marshmallows, chocolate bits, unsweetened chocolate, sweetened shredded coconut.

Such rich and sugary sweets are not for everybody. Fruits are appealing sweets to most adults, especially when sweetened just a bit more than nature has, with honey or brown sugar, or fancied up a bit with crunchy nuts. Perhaps the simplest way to add a special touch to fresh fruit is to make fruit kebabs of cubed bananas, apples, papayas, pineapple, pears, cherries, or grapes. Dip the kebabs into honey thinned with lemon juice. When available, add finely chopped fresh mint to the syrup. Other recipes here demand little more time, and add no more sugar. Even calorie-filled confections, such as cookies and brownies, can be made with wholesome grains.

Frozen Fruit Juice Pops

Fill an ice-cube tray with fruit juice and freeze it. When the juice has begun to solidify, insert a toothpick or ice-cream stick in the center of each cube. Freeze the pops until solid.

Yogurt Fruit Crunch

1 cup plain yogurt or vanilla yogurt
2 tablespoons Almond Granola, p. 2
1 tablespoon honey
Canned pineapple chunks with juice, to taste

Into the yogurt stir the remaining ingredients. Serves 1.

Sautéed Apple Slices

1 firm unpeeled apple, such as a Granny Smith
    or Delicious, cored and cut into 1/4-inch slices
1 1/2 tablespoons butter or margarine
1 tablespoon brown sugar
Cinnamon
Nutmeg

In a skillet melt the butter or margarine and sauté the apple slices for about 5 minutes until they are lightly browned. Turn them, sprinkle them with brown sugar and a dusting of cinnamon and nutmeg, and cook them for about 2 minutes longer. Transfer the slices to a plate and pour the syrup in the skillet over them. Serves 1.

Sautéed Banana

1 large not-too-ripe banana, peeled and sliced in
    half lengthwise
1 tablespoon butter or margarine
1 teaspoon sugar
1 teaspoon light rum
Sour cream

In a skillet melt the butter or margarine and sauté the banana for about 3 minutes until it is lightly browned. Sprinkle the halves with sugar and rum. Do not turn them or they may break. Baste the halves to glaze them. Cook them until they are soft but not mushy. Transfer the halves to a plate, pour the syrup in the skillet over them, and serve with a spoonful of sour cream. Serves 1.

Broiled Grapefruit

1 grapefruit, halved, seeded, and with the sections freed
4 teaspoons dry sherry
4 teaspoons honey

In a small baking pan with a little water in the bottom, put the grapefruit. Drizzle each half with 2 teaspoons dry sherry and 2 teaspoons honey. Broil the halves for a few minutes, until the honey glazes the surface, and is slightly specked with brown. Do not let the honey burn. Serves 2.

Candied Dried Fruit

Dried fruit, such as apricots, peaches, prunes, or mixed dried fruit
Orange juice
1 strip lemon peel

In a saucepan cover the dried fruit with orange juice and add the lemon peel. Over low heat gently simmer the mixture, covered, for 25 to 30 minutes, until the juice is absorbed and the fruit is plumped and glazed. Remove the lemon peel. Serve the fruit warm, or refrigerate it. It will keep for a week, covered.

Chocolate Bread Pudding

1 square unsweetened chocolate
1½ cups milk
2 cups cubed bread, crusts trimmed (about 4 slices)
1 egg, beaten
¼ cup sugar
⅛ teaspoon salt
1 teaspoon vanilla extract
8 large marshmallows, quartered
Cream

In the top part of a double boiler over boiling water melt the chocolate in the milk. Add all the remaining ingredients, except the marshmallows and cream. Cook, stirring frequently, for 5 minutes, or until the mixture is thickened. Fold in the marshmallows and serve warm with cream. Serves 4.

Puffed Pan Cake

Don't mix this batter in a blender or food processor: the egg whites won't rise.

1 cup milk
1 cup flour
⅛ teaspoon salt
3 eggs
1 tablespoon butter or margarine
1 tablespoon sifted confectioners' sugar
2 teaspoons lemon juice

Preheat the oven to 425 degrees. In a bowl mix the milk, flour, and salt. In a separate bowl beat the eggs with a whisk or rotary beater until well blended and frothy. Melt the butter or margarine in a heavy 10-inch skillet with a heatproof handle until it sizzles and remove it from the heat. Quickly mix the eggs into the milk-flour mixture, and pour it into the skillet. Bake on the middle rack of the oven for 15 minutes, or until a cake tester inserted in the center comes out clean. Preheat a separate broiler if you have one. Remove the cake from the oven and light the broiler. Dust the cake with the sugar and sprinkle it with the lemon juice. Put the cake in

To sprinkle a Puffed Pancake evenly with confectioners' sugar, rub the sugar through a sieve with a small spoon.

the broiler until the sugar is caramelized. This is the only tricky part; sugar can burn in the twinkling of an eye. Serve the cake alone or with jam. Serves 6.

Hungarian Pancakes

Crepes, p. 73
Sugar
Apricot jam
Confectioners' sugar
Chopped walnuts

Add 1 teaspoon sugar to the crepe batter and make crepes according to the master recipe.

Preheat the oven to 350 degrees. Spread each crepe with 2 teaspoons apricot jam and roll. Place the crepes, seam side down, in a small baking pan and brush the surfaces with melted butter. Heat the crepes on the middle rack of the oven for 3 to 5 minutes, until the jam is warmed. Sprinkle each crepe with confectioners' sugar and chopped walnuts, and serve.

Oatmeal, Coconut, and Raisin Cookies

> 1 egg
> ¼ teaspoon salt
> ½ teaspoon vanilla extract
> ½ teaspoon baking powder
> ¾ cup firmly packed brown sugar
> ½ cup flour
> 1 tablespoon milk
> 4 tablespoons butter or margarine, melted
> 1 cup oatmeal
> ½ cup packaged sweetened shredded coconut
> ¼ cup raisins

Preheat the oven to 350 degrees. In a deep bowl beat the egg. Add the salt, vanilla, baking powder, brown sugar, flour, and milk and combine. Add the butter or margarine and mix well. Mix in the oatmeal, coconut, and raisins. Drop the batter, a teaspoonful at a time, on greased baking sheets, ½ inch apart. Bake the cookies for 12 minutes, or until the edges are lightly browned. Let them cool on the sheets for a few minutes before removing. Makes 3 dozen.

Scotch Shortbread

Cut this cake into wedges—preferably small ones—while it is still warm. This confection is rich, and disappears fast.

> 1 cup unsalted butter, softened (do not substitute margarine)
> ½ cup confectioners' sugar
> 2 cups sifted flour

Preheat the oven to 375 degrees. In a bowl cream the butter and gradually beat in the sugar. Mix in the flour well. Turn the dough out on a baking sheet and pat it into a circle about ¾ inch thick and 7 inches in diameter. Pinch the edges of the dough and prick it all over with a fork. Bake for 5 minutes, reduce the heat to 300 degrees, and bake for 45 minutes longer. The shortbread should be pale gold, not browned, when ready. Makes 16 small wedges.

Date-Nut Bars

1 cup flour
¼ cup wheat germ
½ teaspoon salt
1 teaspoon baking powder
1 teaspoon cinnamon
1 cup chopped pitted dates
1 cup chopped walnuts
1 cup honey
3 eggs, beaten until thick
¼ cup butter or margarine, melted
Confectioners' sugar

Preheat the oven to 350 degrees. In a large bowl mix the first 5 ingredients. Add the dates and walnuts. In another bowl combine the honey, eggs, and butter or margarine, and stir the mixture into the flour mixture. Mix well and spread the batter evenly in a buttered 9-inch-square baking pan. Bake about 35 minutes, or until a toothpick inserted in the center comes out clean. Let the mixture cool slightly, sprinkle it with the confectioners' sugar, and cut it into bars. Makes about 2 dozen.

Whole-Wheat Brownies

Don't let these super-healthy brownies overbake or they'll be dry. The amount of vanilla may seem excessive, but works out fine with the nutty flavor of whole-wheat flour.

2 squares unsweetened chocolate, broken into pieces
5 tablespoons butter or margarine
⅓ cup cocoa, sifted
¾ cup whole-wheat flour, unsifted
½ teaspoon baking soda
⅛ teaspoon salt
¾ cup turbinado sugar or granulated sugar
¼ cup milk
2 eggs
4 teaspoons vanilla extract
½ cup chopped walnuts (optional)

Preheat the oven to 350 degrees. In a small ovenproof pan combine the chocolate and butter or margarine and transfer it to the oven to melt. In a large bowl combine the cocoa, flour, baking soda, salt, sugar, and milk. In a separate bowl beat the eggs and add the vanilla. With a rubber spatula mix the chocolate mixture into the dry ingredients and stir in the egg mixture. Add the walnuts, if desired. Spread the batter in a buttered 8-inch-square baking pan and bake it on the middle rack of the oven for 20 minutes, or until a toothpick inserted in the center comes out clean. Let the brownies cool for 10 minutes and cut them into 2-inch squares. Makes 16.

S'mores

As every Girl Scout knows, the name derives from the fact that everyone wants "some more." S'mores are traditionally made around the campfire, each person toasting the marshmallows on a stick.

Graham crackers
Chocolate bars
Marshmallows

Put a toasted hot marshmallow and a piece of chocolate between two graham crackers and squeeze gently. (The marshmallow melts the chocolate.) To make indoors, line a baking pan with foil, place marshmallows on it, and broil them until nicely brown. Assemble and eat.

Cereal Chocolate Clusters

How healthy these chocolate clusters are depends on which cereal you use. Consult the label to make your choice. With some supervision, young children can form the bars themselves. Older children should be able to spread the melted chocolate over the shaped bars. For any age, there is a special thrill in producing real "candy" clusters. (You don't have to tell them these chocolate clusters are healthier than those they buy in stores.)

1½ cups puffed rice, puffed wheat, or
  crunchy oat cereal
½ cup dark corn syrup

1 cup chunky peanut butter
¼ cup wheat germ
6 ounces semisweet chocolate bits

In a deep bowl combine the cereal, corn syrup, peanut butter, and wheat germ, mixing gently. Melt the chocolate in a double boiler. Line a jelly-roll pan with waxed paper. Shape fat "clusters" of the cereal mixture with your hands and place them in the pan. When the chocolate is cool but still runny, smooth it over the tops of the clusters, then on the bottom and sides with a table knife, spatula, or fingers. Let the clusters harden in the refrigerator for 30 minutes. Makes 5 or 6.

Adults prefer a knife for spreading lukewarm chocolate, but children may resort to fingers.

Peanut Brittle

1¾ cups shelled roasted peanuts or dry-roasted
  peanuts
⅛ teaspoon salt
2 cups sugar
1 teaspoon butter or margarine

If using roasted peanuts, rub off skins. In a shallow pan lined with buttered waxed paper, spread the peanuts. In a heavy skillet combine the salt and sugar, and heat, stirring frequently, until the sugar has melted and caramelized. Stir in the butter or margarine. Spoon the mixture over the peanuts, spreading it to distribute it evenly. Let the brittle harden and peel it off the waxed paper. Break the brittle into pieces. Makes 1¼ pounds.

ꟷIce-Cream Concoctions

Ingenuity with ice-cream combinations is limited only by the resources of your freezer, refrigerator, and pantry. Experiment with what's on hand, and you may invent a concoction impressive enough to star as the dessert at a future dinner party. Here are a few ideas to start you thinking: crush gingersnaps to fine crumbs with a rolling pin and sprinkle them on orange sherbet, or mix the crumbs into softened sherbet and refreeze. For a sophisticated snack, crush Amaretto cookies or stale macaroons and sprinkle them on vanilla ice cream, then drizzle a spoonful of Amaretto liqueur over the ice cream. Another high-class combo is vanilla ice cream with Hot Fudge Sauce, topped with real whipped cream and garnished with mandarin orange slices and chopped walnuts. Arrange combinations that appeal to the eye as well as the palate, like a Patriot sundae: red raspberry sherbet, vanilla ice cream, and a topping of fresh or frozen and defrosted blueberries. You'll need an array of flavors for the Rainbow, a treat for a crowd of do-it-yourself snackers. Set out cartons of rocky road, pistachio, peach, and cherry ice cream, and lemon, orange, and boysenberry sherbet— or any other colors and flavors that appeal to you. Give everyone a rounded soup spoon or melon baller and let them create their own many colored delights by arranging scoops of whatever flavors they fancy in parfait glasses.

Another thought, albeit a topsy-turvy one, is to use ice cream as the sauce rather than the base of a concoction. Allow vanilla or fruit-flavored ice cream to soften in a bowl, stirring occasionally, until mushy. Spoon it over fresh or frozen fruit.

Butterscotch

You will need a candy thermometer for this recipe. And is that thermometer worth it!

> *2 cups sugar*
> *⅔ cup dark corn syrup*
> *¼ cup water*
> *¼ cup light cream*
> *4 tablespoons butter or margarine*

In a heavy saucepan combine the sugar, corn syrup, water, and cream and stir the mixture as it comes to the boil. Cook, stirring often, until the mixture registers 260 degrees on a candy thermometer. Add the butter or margarine and cook, stirring, until the thermometer registers 280 degrees. Pour the candy into an 8-inch-square pan lined with buttered waxed paper. When the butterscotch is almost set, cut it into squares. When it is cold, break it into pieces. Makes 1¼ pounds.

Hot Fudge Sauce

Use it warm, not really hot. Refrigerated sauce may be reheated over boiling water.

> *2 squares unsweetened chocolate*
> *1 tablespoon butter or margarine*
> *¼ cup boiling water*
> *¾ cup sugar*
> *2 tablespoons light corn syrup*
> *½ teaspoon vanilla extract*
> *2 teaspoons orange liqueur, such as Cointreau,*
> *Grand Marnier, or Curaçao*

In the top of a double boiler melt the chocolate, add the butter, or margarine, and blend. Stir in the boiling water and add the sugar and corn syrup. Place the mixture over direct heat, bring it to a boil, and boil very gently for 7 minutes. Do not stir, or the sauce will become lumpy. Take the sauce off the heat and let it cool slightly. Add the vanilla and the orange liqueur. Makes about 1 cup.

The warmth of Mulled Cider during the holidays.

CHAPTER TEN
Drinks

When you want a between-meal bracer, don't limit yourself to the same old coffee, tea, or cola. The drinks on the following pages range from light to filling, sweet to tart, nutritious to frivolous. There's something for every whim.

To set yourself for a strenuous day, start it off with a blender health drink. It's the painless, digestible, and filling way to get a walloping nutritional blast-off, one that will keep you going until lunchtime. Experiment to find the combination you like. Vary the flavor of your milk base with a few strawberries, half a banana, a peach, some yogurt or a dash of vanilla extract. Try adding other nutritious ingredients or replace the milk with fruit juice. If you're dieting, you'll find that a few ounces of health drink taken at intervals throughout the day may help you to avoid solid food altogether.

Children appreciate drink snacks, too. Reluctant milk drinkers can usually be coaxed with flavored milk; color it pink with grenadine syrup, sweeten it with honey, or give it an ice-cream flavor with a dash of vanilla extract, chocolate, or maple syrup. In winter, prepare flavored gelatin according to directions, but instead of letting the gelatin set, serve it as a hot drink.

Orange Blush

Orange juice
Cranberry juice cocktail
Club soda

Fill a tall glass half full with equal parts orange juice and cranberry juice cocktail. Add ice cubes and fill with club soda. Serves 1.

Mulled Cider

1 quart apple cider
1 2-inch cinnamon stick, broken into pieces
4 whole cloves
¼ cup sugar

In a large saucepan combine all the ingredients and bring to a boil. Cover and simmer the mixture for 10 minutes and strain it. Serve the cider hot and garnish it with additional cinnamon sticks, if desired. Makes 4 to 6 servings.

Banana Slim Shake

1 ripe banana
1 cup skim milk
Vanilla extract or rum extract to taste

In a blender or in a food processor fitted with the metal blade, combine all the ingredients and blend until smooth. Serves 1.

Frullato
(Italian Fruit Whip)

In summertime, these are sold all over Italy at special stands.

⅔ cup milk
⅔ cup fresh berries, such as strawberries or raspberries; or peaches, apricots, pears, or melon, peeled, pitted, and cut into pieces (or frozen unsweetened fruit)
1 to 2 teaspoons sugar
¼ cup crushed ice

In a blender combine all the ingredients and whirl until the ice is melted and the drink is frothy. Serves 1 to 2.

Ginger Buttermilk

> 1 cup buttermilk, chilled
> ¼ cup orange juice, fresh or frozen
> 1 teaspoon lemon juice
> 2 tablespoons firmly packed light brown sugar
> Dash of ground ginger

In a food processor, blender, or with a rotary beater combine all the ingredients and blend them well. Serve in a tall glass. Serves 1.

Ayran
(Turkish Yogurt Drink)

In Turkey, street vendors dispense what looks like small bottles of milk. It isn't milk, though, but ayran.

> Plain yogurt
> Cold water
> Salt to taste

In a glass dilute the yogurt to drinking consistency with water and add salt to taste. Serves 1.

Yogurt-Chocolate Shake

> 1 cup plain yogurt
> ⅓ cup chocolate syrup
> ½ teaspoon vanilla extract
> 2 cups skim milk

In a blender combine all the ingredients and blend them well. Chill and serve in tall glasses. Makes 2⅓ cups.

Floats

Potables and ice cream or sherbet—that's a float. The base is usually a sparkling soft drink or cola, as with the Black Cow: root beer and vanilla ice cream. For a Peppermint Stick, fill a glass with chilled club soda, a scoop of peppermint ice cream, and pop in a peppermint stick for a stirrer. To a glass of ginger ale add a scoop of mint marshmallow ice cream and garnish it with a sprig of mint. Combine strawberry cola with strawberry ice cream, orange soda with orange ice.

Neither a float, a soda, nor a milkshake is the New York City classic, the Egg Cream. The name is a mystery—it contains neither eggs nor cream! Just combine club soda, an equal amount of milk, and a dash of chocolate syrup.

Serve each float with an iced tea spoon for eating the ice cream, but don't expect everybody to use it.

Eggnog

Eggnog is a good hurry-up breakfast. Before bedtime, add a jigger of rum, bourbon, or cognac.

> *1 cup milk, very cold*
> *1 egg*
> *1 tablespoon honey*
> *⅛ teaspoon vanilla extract*
> *Nutmeg, preferably freshly grated*

In a blender combine all the ingredients. Serves 1.

Coffee Drinks

Brew strong, preferably freshly ground coffee for flavorful, vigorous coffee drinks. Since most of the drinks are diluted with milk, cream, or other liquids, you may have to change the proportions you use for ordinary brews. Try one and a half your usual amount of coffee per cup of water. There is no way to successfully reheat leftover coffee without destroying its flavor, but it can be used the same day for cold coffee drinks.

Café au Lait (French Breakfast Coffee)

Simultaneously pour into each cup equal amounts of strong, hot freshly brewed coffee and hot whole milk.

Viennese Coffee

Brew strong coffee, sweeten to taste, and top each cup with whipped cream.

Spiced Dessert Coffee

For 6 servings, brew 6 cups coffee with the seed from 1 cardamom pod. Pour the coffee slowly into tall glasses, having the coffee run down a spoon in the glass to prevent breakage (or heat the glasses first in very hot water). Top each serving with a generous spoonful of whipped cream and a wedge of thinly sliced orange.

Frosted Coffee Hawaii

Combine 2 cups strong cold coffee, 1 cup chilled pineapple juice, and 1 pint coffee ice cream. Whirl in the blender or beat with a rotary beater until the mixture is smooth and foamy. Pour into tall glasses. Serves 4 or 5.

Mocha Frosted

Combine 2 cups cold coffee, ¼ cup chocolate syrup, and 1 pint coffee ice cream. Whirl in a blender or beat with a rotary beater until the mixture is smooth. Pour into tall glasses. Serves 4.

Spiced Iced Coffee

Pour 3 cups very strong hot coffee over 2 sticks cinnamon, 4 whole cloves, and 4 whole allspice berries. Let stand for 1 hour, strain, and pour over ice in 4 tall glasses. Add cream and sugar.

Index